More's *Utopia:* Ideal and Illusion

# More's *Utopia:*
# Ideal and Illusion

by Robbin S. Johnson

New Haven and London, Yale University Press, 1969

# Yale College Series

The tradition of undergraduate writing and publishing has long been a very lively one at Yale, as witnessed by the large number of periodicals, journalistic or literary in character, which have appeared on the Yale campus. These, however, fail to give an accurate picture of the high proportion of good and original scholarly writing which is also done by undergraduates. The excellence of many of the Honors theses written by Yale Seniors made it desirable some years ago to give the most deserving of them the circulation which publication in printed form could provide. Between 1941 and 1957 ten volumes were published in the Undergraduate Prize Essays Series and two in the Scholars of the House Series. The authors of several of these essays have gone on to fulfill amply the promise of their early scholarly efforts. More recently the growing number of theses of outstanding merit has encouraged Yale College and the Yale University Press to establish this new YALE COLLEGE SERIES with the hope that every year it will be possible to publish some of the best work by the Honors majors in the Senior Class. The selection, which is necessarily a very rigorous one, was performed for the Class of 1968 by a faculty committee made up of Messrs. Charles Long, Bruce Russett, and Martin Griffin, Chairman.

Georges May  
Dean of Yale College

# Preface

Thomas More composed his *Utopia* in the years 1515
and 1516. Today, over 450 years later, his book is still
read, still discussed, still alive. Why does such an "out-
dated" work continue to command the interest of so many
people? At first glance More's *Utopia* seems entirely divorced from the peculiar difficulties besetting this genera-
tion. More lived in sixteenth-century England, and the
issues with which he was concerned are not those of our
time: we are not confronted with the threat of an enclosure
movement; our problems are not rooted in a hereditary
monarchical system with its attendant bribery and graft;
and certainly we cannot look for a solution in a dispersed
agricultural community living independently and sep-
arated from its neighbors.

To account for *Utopia's* continued popularity, many
readers have emphasized aspects of the book which support their own particular doctrines or ideologies: com-
munists point to Utopian socialism; Catholics attempt to
read back into *Utopia* More's later religious diatribes;
Protestants attempt to discover a liberal religious atmosphere untainted by More's later disputatious rhetoric. It
is true that More's work includes these issues, but they do
not begin to explain the attraction *Utopia* continues to
hold for its wide audience.

The recurring interest in *Utopia* stems from a more basic characteristic of the work. Before it is a catechism of religious teachings, before it is an ideological dogma, before it is a handbook for sixteenth-century princes, Thomas More's *Utopia* is a discussion of one man's method for balancing the conflicts of the public and private realms. Its fictional narrator, Raphael Hythlodaeus, is the archetype of the utopian visionary. The fictional island-state of Utopia represents the coherent outlines of a *telos* myth. The other characters in the book—Cardinal Morton, Peter Giles, and Thomas More—constitute an audience of learned men acquainted with the real demands of political and private life, men willing to be enchanted by the Utopian fiction but aware that it *is* fiction. In the dialogue among these conflicting personalities with their opposing experiences of life, *Utopia* affirms that the myth of a *telos* is an illusion. Men must govern their ideals; they cannot allow themselves to be governed by them. In *Utopia* Thomas More urges that the value of a utopian myth does not lie in the ends it enshrines but in the means it discloses by which men can introduce true ideals rather than illusory hopes into the real world. Thomas More speaks to us today because he addresses his *Utopia* to the individual conscience, not to the false and misguided hope of a smooth and easy perfection.

The essay which follows attempts to develop this understanding of *Utopia*—that Thomas More is more concerned with defining the proper stance toward the ideals and illusions of a utopian myth than he is with presenting to society a perfected vision of itself. The relations developed in *Utopia* between the author More, the fictional auditor More, and the narrator, Raphael Hythlodaeus, are extremely complex, and their complexity reflects More's desire to plumb the subtle regions of utopianism where ideals shade off into illusions. The very metaphor which More employs to detach himself from Hythlodaeus' Utopian scheme—the metaphor of a play—is much more than a figure of speech. It projects just that rubbing together of fact and fantasy, of reality and illusion, which lies at the frontiers of human expression. *Utopia* argues for an attitude of involvement within detachment, a posture More portrays in the figure of the actor both creating an illusion and measuring the impact of that illusion on his own life. The pages of *Utopia* reveal a man who shares our feelings and hopes yet seeks to be honest with himself and his real world. The enduring image of *Utopia* is not the vision of the perfect state of a commonwealth; rather, it is the reflection of the human spirit struggling to maintain itself before the often overpowering realities of life *and* before the ephemeral fantasies of the mind. This humanistic quest, symbolically represented by the journey to Utopia, is the image of life More addresses to readers of all times.

# Acknowledgments

I wish to acknowledge my profound appreciation of the efforts of Richard S. Sylvester, an educator in the fullest sense and one to whom I owe much more than the few pages which follow. His willingness to give unstintingly of his time and deep knowledge of Thomas More, the contagious enthusiasm and love which he has for the man and his works, the guidance and support he has given me in my pursuit of goals beyond Yale College, all shaped my life in a lasting and rewarding way. I also wish to thank Eugene Waith, who not only stimulated my interest in the Renaissance but also helped to provide the opportunity to broaden my education and range of experiences during a memorable summer in England. The interest he has shown in my activities can only be recognized, never repaid. To my typist must go not only my deepest thanks but also my warmest sympathy for the difficulties in my manuscript with which she had to struggle. Finally, I must thank all those who endured and gave a willing ear to the problems I encountered in writing this essay.

# Contents

# 1

## *Utopia*, the Parerga:
## The Poet and his Audience

Thomas More's *Utopia,* like any masterpiece, has always been and will always remain an elusive work. Confronted with such rich and diffuse material, critics have presented innumerable perspectives on the work, all of which must eventually fail to be definitive. The reader must finally content himself not with defining the final meaning of *Utopia* but with allowing the methods and suggestions of the book to illuminate his own mind, his own perceptions, his own life. Such a response to the work suggests an interesting, though obviously incomplete, characterization of More's *Utopia:* in it More has translated into verbal images and an intelligible semantic structure ideas the origins of which lie in the fantasies and dreams of an alert, mature mind. Characterizing the work in this manner ignores many of its possible dimensions, but it does serve to call attention to certain very real aspects of *Utopia.*

More's "best state of a commonwealth"[1] *(De Optimo*

---

1. *The Yale Edition of the Complete Works of St. Thomas More,* Vol. 4: *Utopia,* ed. Edward Surtz, S.J., and J. H. Hexter (New Haven, 1965), p. 47. All quotations from *Utopia* itself are taken from this edition, and page references for them are incorporated directly into my text. References to the Commentary and Introductions of the editors will be cited in the footnotes as *Utopia.*

*Statu Respublicae)* evolved through several stages of composition: first came the Discourse on Utopia (what is now
Book II), which More wrote in 1515; later, in London
during the winter of 1515–16, More added the "Dialogue
of Counsel" and the dialogue-within-a-dialogue set at Cardinal Morton's table (these two dialogues are now Book I);
finally, More solicited the responses to his work of humanist friends and added two letters himself (these letters, with
some variation, were joined to the editions of *Utopia).*[2]
By considering *Utopia* in the context of this evolving creative process, one may gain some insight into how Thomas
More developed his relationship to the themes and mean-
ings he saw emerging in his work. The above three literary
"moments" or phases of *Utopia,* then, represent not only
More's complete accomplishment but also provide a means
of at least outlining how he employed the idea of a utopian
myth to illuminate his own life. By accompanying More
into the realm of the fantastic through these separate
phases, the reader pushes to the source of *Utopia's* elusive-
ness: he comes to see the work as a personal exploration
made universal; he begins to look into the symbolic processes of More's mind as well as of his own.

The most concise presentation of these three phases as a
means of analyzing More's *Utopia* systematically is Berger's:

> The relations which determine the overall structure of
> *Utopia* are after all primarily verbal, intelligible and
> temporal: the three moments which unfold its experi-
> ence are relatively discrete units, each more condensed
> and immediate than those which follow it. The letter to

2. See J. H. Hexter, *Utopia: The Biography of an Idea* (Princeton,
1965), or *Utopia,* pp. xv-xxiii, for a concise presentation of the sequence
of composition of More's *Utopia.*

Giles frames both parts of the work within the present tense of the writer's experience, while the first book frames Hythloday's monologue in the more realistic and inclusive context of European affairs. The openness and intimacy of More's address to Peter Giles establishes the proper distance for the reader, who is in effect the addressee. Such places of the mind as Hythloday's green world are best dealt with not in lonely voyages but in the friendly play of an afternoon's talk, in the good fellowship of men who love and trust each other, in the shared discourse which refreshes weary minds so that they can return to the stage of the actual world next morning.[3]

This tripartite division should be qualified by the addition to the first category of More's second letter to Peter Giles. These three compositional phases bear some interesting and suggestive relations to each other. The first phase (the two letters to Giles) was the last written; the second phase was composed between the other two; phase three was the first section to be composed. Moreover, the first phase is the most immediate in terms of More's relationship to his audience; in it he speaks directly to the reader as the "addressee." Phase two is distanced into a dialogue presented before the reader. Phase three is the most remote, for it is a monologic narrative which is first related to More and then retold by him to the reader. Phase one is the most immediate section in a rhetorical sense as well: More's style is directly explanatory. In the second phase the dialogue intervenes between the reader and the participants, and the reader must make some evaluations of the characters and their stands. The third phase is the most complex rhetorically. Hythlodaeus presents Utopia to

3. Harry Berger, Jr., "The Renaissance Imagination: Second World and Green World," *The Centennial Review, 9* (Winter 1965), 71.

More from a conviction that it is praiseworthy, and he is forceful in emphasizing what he considers should be praised. More records Hythlodaeus' narrative for the reader. In doing so, however, he introduces a second perspective, one which must function implicitly, yet which demands that the reader recognize that More, the mediating poet, may respond to Utopia and her institutions differently than the narrator-guide, Raphael Hythlodaeus. Finally, the first phase is the most immediate in content; it is developed by a real man in a real world facing real problems. Phase two takes up the confrontation between the real person (More) and the philosopher (Hythlodaeus) who brings to the real world an ideal scheme of things. The third phase takes the reader and the mediating poet to this ideal world, sets them afoot in it, and guides them through its kaleidoscopic ideality.

This essay will analyze *Utopia* in these three phases. My underlying assumption is that Thomas More intended that the reader understand them not as they evolved temporally but as they finally stand. Though the reader must remain aware of how *Utopia* was born, he should ultimately attempt to see the work as the finished product More presented to his humanist contemporaries. Therefore, the present chapter will discuss the first phase of *Utopia,* the final and most immediate aspects of More's efforts. The second chapter will deal with the intermediate phase—the dialogues of Book I. Chapter 3 will review the narrative of *Utopia*—Book II—in the perspective of the two preceding phases, and Chapter 4 will attempt to summarize the meaning of the utopian myth for Thomas More as it seems to emerge from his finished work.

The first phase, the parerga and especially More's two letters to Peter Giles, deals with several of the interpretative problems of *Utopia* directly, and it is perhaps a testimonial to More's recognition of the complexity of his book that he suggests some guidelines to understanding his meaning. One problem with which he deals in these letters is the question of how man defines his personality and his personal relationship to the real world. More's conduct in his public as well as his private affairs contrasts sharply with the remoteness, the noninvolvement with life of Hythlodaeus. Raphael's detachment from the present is suggested by his absence. Twice in his first letter More asks Peter Giles to attempt to reach Raphael either "by word of mouth or by letter" (41, 43). In the second letter, More tells those who doubt the veracity of his account to go and search out "Hythlodaeus himself, for he is not yet dead. I heard lately from travelers coming from Portugal that on last March first he was as hale and spirited as ever" (251–53). The news of Raphael is indirect and second hand; one does not really have the man, only his ideas.

Even these ideas, More suggests, are remote, for they are "the product of a person who, as you know, was not so well acquainted with Latin as with Greek" (39). As Berger remarks, a preoccupation with Greek at the expense of Latin is a convention frequently used by Renaissance humanists to express a contrast between philosophic isolation and a more pragmatic and immediate civil involvement. "Unable to control his distance and detachment within the world, he [Hythlodaeus] detaches himself from the world. (More, like Alberti and other humanists, indicates this tendency by remarking Hythloday's preference for Greek over Latin.)"[4] Thus, Hythlodaeus is remote not only physically but also intellectually, a man coming from and going to a world of detached philosophic idealism.

4. Berger, p. 63.

In contrast to this image of a detached Raphael, More presents a portrait of himself as overburdened by his full participation in life:

> I am constantly engaged in legal business, either pleading or hearing, either giving an award as arbiter or deciding a case as judge. I pay a visit of courtesy to one man and go on business to another. I devote almost the whole day in public to other men's affairs and the remainder to my own. I leave to myself, that is to learning, nothing at all. (39)

The last sentence seems to argue that law is diverting Thomas More from other more important studies. To conclude from this that More hated the legal profession and saw it as antithetical to his humanistic interests would be to misconstrue the evidence. The Lincoln's Inn records show that Thomas More continued to serve actively in the affairs of the institution where he was trained. His commitments of time and energy to the law suggest that he found something of great importance in it—the lesson of how to live in this world without being of it.[5] More's relationship to the law portrays a mediating stance which Raphael is incapable of understanding—a suspension between the real world and the hope of some ideal.

More's commitments to the real world extend beyond the affairs of business to his family, friends, and servants:

> When I have returned home, I must talk with my wife, chat with my children, and confer with my servants. All this activity I count as business when it must be

5. R. J. Schoeck, "Thomas More, Lawyer and Judge," the second of three *St. Thomas More Lectures,* delivered at Yale University, Dec. 4, 1967.

done—and it must be unless you want to be a stranger in your own home. Besides, one must take care to be as agreeable as possible to those whom nature has supplied, or chance has made, or you yourself have chosen, to be the companions of your life, provided you do not spoil them by kindness, or through indulgence make masters out of your servants. (39–41)[6]

All of these duties—business, affairs of the household, and the demands of friends—come before the writing of *Utopia*. This system of priorities does not mean that art should be valued below many of the pedestrian facts of life; rather, it draws attention to the relation of art to life. The values of each are important, and lessons from them interpenetrate. Hythlodaeus draws his strength from his philosophic ideals alone; he can brook no interference from other claims.[7] More affirms that the human person-

6. The family, both in Thomas More's life and in *Utopia,* is very important. In the sixteenth century, the family was a rather large unit, often including several generations, many relatives by marriage, and apprentices or servants. "The master-apprentice relationship of the guilds involved ideally a quasi-familial connection, the master standing *in loco parentis* to his apprentices. In keeping with the emphasis on the family in Utopia, More goes further by bringing the apprentice into a practically filial relationship to the master" (*Utopia,* p. 403). More himself served in the household of Cardinal Morton, and, as Chambers observes, "there can be no doubt as to the very great advantages More derived" from this experience (R. W. Chambers, *Thomas More* [Ann Arbor, Mich., 1962], p. 60). In contrast to More's regard for the affections traditional in the family, Hythlodaeus' relation to his family (55) seems very irresponsible. Raphael's lack of concern for family intimacy partially explains the sometimes callous way he pictures the Utopian household (115, 137).

7. As More notes at the very end of *Utopia,* "I was not quite certain that he could brook any opposition to his views, particularly when I recalled his censure of others on account of their fear that they might not appear to be wise enough, unless they found some fault to criticize in other men's discoveries" (245). This truculence derives not merely

ality straddles two worlds—the realm of people as well as the realm of ideas.

Beyond this image of life's complexity lies an even more informative statement: *Utopia,* to a large extent, was born out of this mixed quality of life and should finally be understood as reflecting upon the problems posed by the overlapping claims of life and art.

> When, then, can we find time to write? Nor have I spoken a word about sleep, nor even of food, which for many people takes up as much time as sleep—and sleep takes up almost half a man's life! So I get for myself only the time I filch from sleep and food. Slowly, therefore, because this time is but little, yet finally, because this time *is* something, I have finished *Utopia.* (41)

In reviewing the ground from which *Utopia* has grown—this active and real world of business, family, and familiar ritual—More suggests that utopian ideas can find their true place in life only when they are adjusted to the impinging demands of reality. This letter to Giles implies that the ultimate facts which called up *Utopia,* which qualified its meaning for More, which defined its final outlines, were not the rationally coherent facts of Hythlodaeus' Utopian social theory but life's common features considered in the illuminating light of More's experience, his consciousness of duty, and his understanding of right action done in good conscience.

From this personal perspective on *Utopia* More proceeds to a more abstract consideration of the relevance of

---

from a mental commitment to his ideals; it also results from Hythlodaeus' total identification with his ideas, making any doubt, in effect, a denial of his very being.

Utopian themes to life. The introduction into this more abstract level begins with the problem of the width of the bridge which spans the river Anydrus. Even such a simple detail raises the question of the meaning of objectivity and truth in the work.

> If you do not remember [the length of the bridge], I shall put down, as I have actually done, what I myself seem to remember. Just as I shall take great pains to have nothing incorrect in the book, so, if there is doubt about anything, I shall rather tell an objective falsehood than an intentional lie—for I would rather be honest than wise. (41)[8]

The idea of an objective falsehood suggests another concept—a false objectivity, a negative reality. Utopian society is neither real nor objectively described. In fact, Utopia (Nowhere) is a negative ideal which Hythlodaeus attempts to make real and positive. The very terms of this inversion become self-negating.

> Thus, if I had done nothing else than impose names on ruler, river, city, and island such as might suggest to the more learned that the island was nowhere, the city a phantom, the river without water, and the ruler without a people, it would not have been hard to do and would have been much wittier than what I actually did. (251)

8. The marginal gloss suggests that a "theological distinction" is being made here, "but the distinction does not seem to appear in moral guides by Aquinas, Antoninus, and Silvester, or even by a later authority like Alphonsus Ligouri." Rather, the important distinction is between honesty and wisdom. More himself testifies that he is not so "superstitiously veracious, as to shrink from a fib"—or, perhaps, from a literary jeu d'esprit which may be misleading—if some more important values may thus be expressed (*Utopia,* pp. 291–92).

What More actually does, of course, is give to these facts names which reveal to the learned reader that Utopia is a fiction.[9] Thus, Hythlodaeus is placed in the ironic literary situation of trying to transform fiction into reality, the negative into the positive, nothing into truth. In fact, since he has embodied this ideal in his own personality (which also does not exist, for he, like his ideal, is only a fiction), he pushes reality from both ends into the limbo of the fantastic. It is against this ironic self-immolation that Raphael's claim to have discovered the true ideal must be measured.

Hythlodaeus' Utopia negates its meaning and image on yet another level. Not only is a fictional character attempting to represent a fiction as reality; the false world he offers Europe is emasculated, soft, an unreal paradise of unearned pleasures.

Utopia is a Platonic Garden of Adonis, a place without pain where everyone learns everything the short smooth way: "amonge the Utopians, where all things be sett in good order," time has no function and history no meaning. The hard-won accomplishments of Western culture are absorbed without sweat or struggle; Utopian logic and imagination replace the trial-and-error of human experience. The Utopians are handed the classical inheritance in the Aldine edition, untrammeled by the existential context of past-and-present, loss-and-recovery, which has made that inheritance so precious.[10]

9. Explanations of these names may be found in the Commentary of *Utopia:* for "Utopus" and "Utopia," see p. 385; for "Amaurotum," see p. 388; for "Anydrus," see p. 392.

10. Berger, p. 68. Peter Giles' last misgiving about Utopia and Raphael's response to his doubts help to place the values which may be gained from Hythlodaeus' Utopian tale in their proper perspective.

Thus, Utopian "truth" proves doubly false. On the one hand, Utopia (Nowhere) is negative, unreal, because her citizens are a fiction and her prophet-philosopher is fictional. On the other hand, "Eutopia" ("the happy place") reveals itself as a garden of illusory, empty pleasures, pleasures gained without struggle or sacrifice. Because it does not share in the history of man, Raphael's Utopia becomes the Nowhere of the mind, the negative essence of life. The reader is called away from Hythlodaeus' fantasy world and back to the existential origins of *Utopia* in those hours More "filches" from sleep and food, those hours spaced between life's everyday demands which qualify the utopian myth and to which More brings the ideal vision in order to amplify his existence and to inform it with an ideal wish.

The final problem More deals with in these letters is the nature of his audience. The question of audience is important for establishing the ultimate province of the utopian myth. The audience to whom *Utopia* is directed is

---

Giles argues that one should not disparage the struggles (and the adventures) involved in Europe's continued efforts to cope with life: "long experience has come upon very many advantages for human life —not to mention also the chance discoveries made among us, which no human mind could have devised" (107). Raphael replies: "just as they immediately at one meeting appropriated to themselves every good discovery of ours, so I suppose it will be long before we adopt anything that is better arranged with them than with us" (109). Surtz is correct in observing that by this interchange "More wishes to inculcate a receptiveness and an open-mindedness toward new ideas or, at least, toward better ways of doing things" (*Utopia*, p. 383). But, in view of the value which Peter Giles assigns to experience, one should not leap totally to the Utopian manner of assimilating everything "immediately at one meeting." More and the reader must strike a balance between Raphael's suggestive idealism and the truth of experience: nothing is either precious or ultimately real which comes without effort, which is not placed in the historical context of loss-and-recovery.

made explicit in the second letter: "But I should certainly have tempered the fiction so that, if I wanted to abuse the ignorance of common folk, I should have prefixed some indications at least for the more learned to see through our purpose" (251). Unlike many "political" treatises of the time (Erasmus' *Education of a Christian Prince,* Machiavelli's *The Prince,* and others), *Utopia* is not intended ultimately for the instruction of rulers.[11] The subtle revelation of its fictional character through the names, and the consequent irony which develops, demand an audience of men trained in literature, acquainted with the classics, and profoundly sensitive to the elusive tone of many of its passages. Equally as curious as the notion of a "political" treatise for nonpoliticians is More's disparagement of the "common folk." In the first letter this disparagement grows to extended and deeply pessimistic denouncement of their ability ever to comprehend *Utopia.* After a long attack on their barbarity, insensitivity, dull-mindedness, and jealousy, More addresses his book directly: "Go now and provide a feast at your own expense for men of such dainty palate, of such varied taste, and of such unforgetful and grateful natures!" (45). The reader can only be puzzled

11. The men to whom *Utopia* is directed, the men whose opinions More was eager to hear (men like Busleyden and Giles), are persons with some practical experience in government. Busleyden was employed in several governmental roles (*Utopia,* p. 279); Giles held, at the time of More's writing of *Utopia,* a "high position in his home town" (49). But they were not, in any sense, "princes." Like More at this time (1516), they are first of all learned men, and their main interest in politics derives from their hopes of defining a means to good conduct and a sound commonwealth and from their relatively detached perspective on how to achieve these humanist ends. Though they are men interested in outlining sound rules for governing people, because they are not "princes" they are sensitive to an exploratory and tentative treatise on government. To them, *Utopia* is not a handbook but an examination of the impact of their humanist ideals on the patterns of life and government they see on all sides.

by this extreme pessimism and intentional obscurity unless he identifies in it a substantive meaning. In effect, More seems to be concluding that the full complexity of the relation of the utopian ideal to life can be understood only by a few and can be comprehended, in the larger sense of being incorporated into an individual's life, only by those very few who have struggled to acquire knowledge in a world which seems to militate against any but the most foolish and rash conduct. In order to make more precise what More means by thus restricting his audience, it is necessary to examine the concept of utopianism and the personal use to which Renaissance humanists often put their irony.

The myth of utopia embraces both man and society. It attempts to join them in an ideal union. When considering society the myth seeks to define the common cause which will bind all men together. When considering man it faces the problem of how an individual is to give his life meaningful content by relating it to a larger whole. Thus, the utopian view of man and society is essentially paradoxical: on the one hand, it must view life as a social aggregate, as an institutional pattern; on the other hand, it must view life as an aggregate of unique persons, as a pattern of individual aspirations. The paradox arises in that these two ends —the institutional and the individual—are mutually exclusive in the real world.

That personal fulfillment comes only as the individual loses himself in a preoccupation with some social goal beyond himself is a truth which has been recognized by moral and mental theorists for centuries. But this truth cannot without unconscionable risk be made the foundation of a political philosophy. Considering the difficulty of finding men who can be trusted not to abuse the relatively modest function of insuring the reciprocal freedom of citizens to choose and follow their own separate goals, it is fatuous to suppose that any leader, elite group, or majority of men is so virtuous and wise as to qualify for the task of choosing goals to which all shall be compelled to give allegiance.[12]

Since it acknowledges that man achieves fulfillment only by dedicating himself to a larger ideal, the utopian myth must either focus upon the goal to the exclusion of the individual effort to achieve self-expression or sanctify the aspiring individual to the exclusion of the common cause. The traditional integrated or institutional *telos* ideals and the traditional individualistic aspirations thus become, ironically, irreconcilable.

Both the institutional and the individual manifestations of the utopian ideal derive ultimately from man's dreams of a better life. "The desire for a state of perfect repose and life eternal has always haunted mankind, and poets have forever been the spokesmen for the dream."[13] Three components make up this utopian tradition: man's propensity to dream of a better state; the state itself, which is seen as realizing this dream; and the poet who records the two. Clearly, the institutionalization of the utopian *telos* begins as the dream is transformed into a social theory which man sees as the answer to his hopes. Lewis Mumford has suggested that we examine the possible historical genesis of the utopian ideal in order to understand the dream of a perfect state when it achieves institutional expression:

12. R. V. Andelson, "Where Society's Claim Stops," *American Journal of Economics and Sociology,* 27 (January 1968), 53.
13. A. Bartlett Giamatti, *The Earthly Paradise and the Renaissance Epic* (Princeton, 1966), p. 3.

Though I have long been a student of both utopias and cities, only in recent years have sufficient data come to light to suggest to me that the concept of Utopia is not a Hellenic speculative fantasy, but a derivation from an historic event: that indeed the first utopia was the city itself. If I can establish this relationship, more than one insight should flow from it: not least an explanation of the authoritarian nature of so many utopias.[14]

In effect Mumford is arguing that the leap from a hunting and gathering culture to a city-based culture seemed, to the people of that time, the realization of their dreams of a utopian *telos*. Though the ultimate source of the ideal remains in the imagination, transforming the myth into an historic event recreates, as an institution, what before was merely a vague wish.

The human imagination was willing to accept the city as a realization of its utopian dreams, Mumford argues, because of the city's apparently divine origin.

This cosmic orientation, these mythic-religious claims, this royal preemption of the powers and functions of the community are what transformed the mere village or town into a city: something "out of this world," the home of a god. Much of the contents of the city— houses, shrines, storage bins, ditches, irrigation works —was already in existence in smaller communities: but though these utilities were necessary antecedents of the city, the city itself was transmogrified into an ideal form —a glimpse of eternal order, a visible heaven on earth, a seat of life abundant—in other words, utopia.[15]

14. Lewis Mumford, "Utopia, The City and The Machine," *Daedalus, 94* (Spring 1965), 271.
15. Ibid., p. 281.

The origin of the city in a mythic-religious act transforms the common institutions of life into perfected expressions of man's dreams. The first historic city seemed to be what man had dreamed about; the city seemed to be truly "the seat of life abundant."

Not only did the lowliest subject have a direct glimpse of heaven in the setting of the temple and the palace, but with this went a secure supply of food, garnered from the nearby fields, stored under guard in the granary of the citadel, distributed by the temple. The land itself belonged to the god or the king, as it still does ultimately in legal theory to their abstract counterpart, the sovereign state; and the city forecast its literary successor in treating the land and its agricultural produce as a common possession: fair shares, if not equal shares, for all.[16]

This city was also the seat of equality among men. The king or state owns all the land and uses it for the benefit of the common interest; all produce is distributed by the state, and shares, if not equal, are parceled out as needed. In this historic realization of the utopian ideal, community of property stood at the core.

Unfortunately, to keep the ideal alive and community of property at its center required "another daring invention of kingship: the collective human machine, the platonic model of all later machines."[17] In other words, the utopia became fact only through an inhuman and pervasive coercion.

16. Ibid., p. 282.
17. Ibid., p. 283.

By royal command, the necessary machine was created: a machine that concentrated energy in great assemblages of men, each unit shaped, graded, trained, regimented, articulated, to perform its particular function in a unified working whole.

The utopian ideal gave birth to the depersonalized human machine, and community of property extended to the individual human being. Discipline of the most coercive and dictatorial kind thus became associated with communism, for the discipline was not a willing and mutual submission to larger social goals by the citizens but the decree of the prince, whose first concern was preserving the state.

When this ideal was transformed into a verbal image and a philosophic unity, discipline became not only unilateral and externally imposed rather than mutual and willing; it also became a permanent coercion.

From the first, a kind of mechanical rigidity afflicts all utopias. On the most generous interpretation, this is due to the tendency of the mind, or at least of language, noted by Bergson, to fix and geometricize all forms of motion and organic change: to arrest life in order to understand it, to kill the organism in order to control it, to combat that ceaseless process of self-transformation which lies at the very origin of species.[18]

In other words, the mythical tradition of the utopian ideal which grew from the historical event amplified the institutional coercion inherent in the ideal by eliminating all processes of social change. The image of utopia (as opposed to the aspiring spirit to which it was originally a

18. Ibid., p. 275.

testimonial) became divorced from reality. Achieving the
ideal entailed the destruction of the organism whose life
was its end. The utopian ideal turned back upon itself and
made its realization death.

If institutionalizing the utopian ideal ends with the common interest tyrannizing over the benefits of each individual member, the individual utopian dreamer, considered
alone, tends to withdraw from any socially common cause.
He merges his own being into the ideal which he envisions
rather than into the general hopes of men. Raphael Hythlodaeus expresses this apotheosis of the utopian individual
in an anecdote which he draws from Plato:

> "For this reason, Plato by a very fine comparison shows
> why philosophers are right in abstaining from adminis-
> tration of the commonwealth. They observe the people
> rushing out into the streets and being soaked by con-
> stant showers and cannot induce them to go indoors and
> escape the rain. They know that, if they go out, they can
> do no good but will only get wet with the rest. Therefore,
> being content if they themselves at least are safe, they
> keep at home, since they cannot remedy the folly of
> others." (103)[19]

19. The anecdote reveals how philosophic detachment involves the
loss of any sense of personal responsibility; the home to which the
philosopher keeps is the safe and easy idealism of the mind's rational
theorizing. The same anecdote occurs in More's correspondence, and
the interpretation which he gives it is strikingly different from that
which Hythlodaeus presents. See *The Correspondence of Sir Thomas
More,* ed. Elizabeth Frances Rogers (Princeton, 1947), pp. 512–13,
518–20. Though, as Chambers notes in a comment added by Miss
Rogers (514), one cannot be absolutely certain that More is the actual
author of the letter in which the anecdote appears, the words are characteristic of him. In this letter ("Margaret Roper to Alice Alington,
August 1534," pp. 514–32), More first recalls Wolsey's use of the fable
of the wise men retreating into their caves: Wolsey employs it to

When the utopian dream moves away from society and toward the individual, it turns all expression inward. The dream itself, and not the social characteristics of the dream, becomes all-important. This internalizing effect caused by the ability to envision utopia should not be confused with the character of the state imagined. Internalizing the dream is a psychological phenomenon independent of the philosophic content of the *telos* envisioned. One may easily individualize the impact of the utopian myth while still defining that myth as an institutional ideal. Indeed, part of the purpose of this essay will be to demonstrate that what makes Hythlodaeus' Utopia unacceptable is its coercive institutionalism and self-serving idealism. The point to be made is that this

---

prove that England would be wise to go to war to avoid having all the fools of Europe band together against her (518). More concludes: "But whome soeuer my Lorde [Wolsey] meaneth for the wyse men, and whomsoeuer his Lordeship take for the fooles, and who[m]soeuer longe for the rule, and who so euer longe for none, I besech our Lorde make vs all so wyse as that we may euery man here so wiselie rule our selfe in this time of teares, this vale of mysery, this simple wretched worlde . . . God, I say, geue vs the grace so wisely to rule our self here, that when we shall hence in hast to mete the great Spouse, we be not taken sleapers and for lacke of light in our lampes, shit out of heauen among the v. folish vyrgins" (519–20). In other words, after concluding that the supposedly wise philosophers actually acted very foolishly in retreating to their caves (519), yet not agreeing with Wolsey's use of the anecdote as a call to arms, More transforms the fable into a metaphorical lesson which is meant to instruct each man to govern wisely his own kingdom—his conscience.

More interprets this fable in response to a request by Alice Alington who, when she inquired of the then Lord Chancelor (Sir Thomas Audley) whether he would "be goode lorde vnto my father [Thomas More—see 512] whan he sawe his tyme" (513), reported that Audley had replied "I woulde not haue your father so scrupulous of his conscience" (513), citing Aesop's fable of the wise men retreating into their caves as evidence for the foolishness of attempting to avoid the common attitudes of men.

psychological individualizing of an institutional ideal in no way bridges the gap which the utopian *telos* myth creates between man and society. The content of the myth institutionalizes the ideal by devaluing the individual; but the philosopher equates his personal expression, his personality, with the ideal he envisions. In either case, the individual is ultimately lost to the institutional ideal: when the utopian *telos* myth is realized, the individual self is consumed by the common cause, by the institutions of Utopia; and when the utopian *telos* myth is visualized, the individual who conceives the ideal submerges his whole personality in the philosophic perfection he has seen. The paradox of the utopian myth is inescapable; there seems to be no way to preserve the individual against the tyranny of utopia's social idealism. Whether considered as an institutional ideal or an individual's idealism the irony remains the same: defining utopia means destroying the individual organism it originally was meant to serve.

But we must finally consider the mediator between the ideal and the individual—the poet. As a mediator the poet must come to grips with the demands of an ideal both upon social conduct and upon the individual mind. He must balance a consciousness of life's demands with a consciousness of life's ideals and the dictates of the community's conscience with the dictates of the individual's conscience.[20] As Sylvester notes, Roper's biography of

20. Hythlodaeus and his Utopian ideal both seek to make a concern for the general welfare the normal pattern of behavior. "Even though the rules of private ownership under carefully specified conditions may be legitimate and therefore worthy of observance, they cannot provide 'the best order of a commonwealth,' which is the theme of *Utopia,* because they make concern with the common welfare seem a work of supererogation, a matter of 'devotion' rather than of duty and habit" (*Utopia,* p. 450). Nowhere is the danger of the ease and convenience underlying Hythlodaeus' ideal more clearly expressed, for to eliminate the element of "devotion" in working for the general welfare is to

Thomas More dramatically illustrates how More bridged the gap between the outer and inner worlds through a unique and disciplined consciousness-in-conscience:

> We have to be very careful with this word "Conscience" in sixteenth-century literature. While its modern meaning was well-established in More's day, the word also retained its older sense (now completely lost); etymologically, "Conscience" is a "knowing with," a special awareness that we can perhaps paraphrase best as "consciousness," a full sensitivity to oneself and to the world about one.[21]

This full sensitivity enabled More to uphold the ideals of his inner being without withdrawing completely from the affairs which surrounded him; it enabled him to live in the

---

eliminate a predicament essential to the human character—man's limited means placed against unlimited demands, a situation which makes choice and sacrifice necessary. More's letters to Giles again and again express his acute sense of this predicament. To argue that More agrees with Hythlodaeus, to conclude that More wishes to eliminate the sense of human fulfillment derived from acts of "supererogation" (doing more than duty requires), is to deny the awareness of life's demands More has just expressed so cogently. Thus, More's role as the mediating poet becomes clear: he is attempting to strike a balance between Hythlodaeus' negation of the necessity to sacrifice and the nihilistic feeling (a tone which seems to intrude into some moments of these letters to Giles) that the choice of one avenue precludes any other alternative. More must make a concern for the common good the natural product of man's humanness without destroying either the sense of self-fulfillment implied in a willing choice or the recognition that dedication to mankind testifies to the reciprocal dimension of human freedom.

21. This quotation is taken from the text of a lecture by Richard S. Sylvester, originally delivered at a San Francisco symposium on Aug. 13, 1965, p. 9. The text will be published under the title "Detachment and Involvement in the World of Thomas More."

world without being consumed by it, to compromise with its traditions without compromising his ardent striving toward an ennobled and religious life.

What More accomplished through consciousness-in-conscience many of the Renaissance humanists achieved through a related attitude—a self-comprehension through irony. The liberating effect of this attitude enabled Erasmus, for example, to create his *Praise of Folly:*

> It will be observed that one of the great virtues of this kind of irony, which might be called the irony of complexity, is its opposition to dogmatism. By means of it Erasmus is able to examine in all its difficult complications a central human problem: the relation between comfortable conformity and the painful independence of wisdom. We are convinced, consequently, that his choice is neither that of a dreamy idealist nor of a rigid moralist. It is a kind of irony consonant with Erasmus' character and with the common quality of most forms of Renaissance humanism, namely, that attitude towards life which is comprehensive and flexible without being irresponsible.[22]

Erasmus employs this ironic method to validate the arduous wisdom of his choice as he pursues learning in a world where foolishness reigns and learning goes unappreciated. More, as the poet of *Utopia,* faces a different problem: how to balance social wisdom not only against the foolish and corrupt practices of men in real life but also against the tantalizing urge to retreat into the illusory world of theoretical perfection.

22. Leonard F. Dean, "Literary Problems in More's *Richard III,*" *PMLA, 58* (1943), 31–32.

The first adjustment which this consciousness of the poet makes over the psychologically unconscious commitment of the idealist to his utopian myth is to differentiate between the *telos* myth as theory and as fantasy. "The utopia is a *speculative* myth; it is designed to contain or provide a vision for one's social ideas, not to be a theory connecting social facts together."[23] To recognize that the utopian myth is fantasy, not theory, is crucial if the poet is to free himself from Raphael's total psychological commitment to the ideal. Hythlodaeus can see in Utopia only a rational and coherent social theory, and, since he hopes to rationalize human conduct, the way is open for him to leap immediately to the ideal represented by the Utopians. He is unable to see the Utopians as they really are—a fiction. They become for him like the city for the men of the Age of Pyramids—a reality, a historic event. He loses all sense of proportion, of distance, of perspective, and becomes wholly subsumed into this seemingly ideal fact. As a result of this immersion in the rationalism of his ideal society he makes a fatal mistake: he confuses the appearance of reason with reasonable reality—a confusion which is almost conventional in literary utopias:

> The procedure of constructing a utopia produces two literary qualities which are typical, almost invariable, in the genre. In the first place, the behavior of society is described *ritually.* . . . In the second place, rituals are apparently irrational acts which become *rational* when their significance is explained. . . . It is a common objection to utopias that they present human nature as governed more by reason than it is or can be. But this

23. Northrup Frye, "Varieties of Literary Utopias," *Daedalus, 94* (Spring 1965), 323.

rational emphasis, again, is the result of using certain literary conventions. The utopian romance does not present society as governed by reason; it presents it as governed by ritual habit, or prescribed social behavior, which is explained rationally.[24]

What Hythlodaeus does when describing what he saw in Utopia, and especially in describing the function of community of property in this society, is to rationalize all human conduct. He presents a coherent theory which ties all social rituals together in a unified whole. The truly fantastic thrust of *Utopia* is much less integrated, much less coherent, for it approaches a society not as a system of institutions and patterns of ritual behavior but as an assemblage of men. Theory assumes that there exists a logical social goal around which all conduct may be organized. The fantasy of *Utopia* begins with the recognition that "it is fatuous to suppose that any leader, elite group, or majority of men is so virtuous and wise as to qualify for the task of choosing goals to which all shall be compelled to give allegiance."[25] What differentiates theory from fantasy, Hythlodaeus from More, in *Utopia,* is that theory declares that community *is* society's goal; fantasy only urges that it *should be.* The consciousness of the difference between social theory and social fantasy enables the poet to perform his mediating role. He perceives Hythlodaeus' involvement in the Utopian ideal from a detached position and thus is able to see that the coherent rationalism of Utopian social theory is actually an imaginary attribute produced by the mesmerizing attractiveness of the ideal. Theory demands, and receives, Hythlodaeus' full commitment; fantasy demands, to some extent, suspending

24. Ibid., pp. 324–25.
25. Andelson, p. 53.

disbelief and engaging the mind, but it also, and finally, makes the mind aware that what is seen is only suggestive, not definitive.

This consciousness of utopian myth as fantasy, however, presupposes an antecedent awareness—a recognition of the utopian ideal as myth. At a time when myths were taken as facts, the individual consciousness may well have thought the union between life and the ideal to be imminently possible. Indeed, it is this very spirit which channels the human imagination into mythological expression. When the myth finally becomes recognized as fiction and not reality, the union no longer seems possible unless another myth, a myth which suggests a means by which to bridge this gap, is born. In the seventeenth century such a myth (the myth of progress) arose out of the emerging hopes for gradual technological mastery over the human environment.

And because technology is progressive, getting to the utopia has tended increasingly to be a journey in time rather than space, a vision of the future and not of a society located in some isolated spot on the globe.[26]

The myth of progress transposes a spatial into a temporal metaphor, transfers the remote or peripheral to the imminent and terminal. What once was only possible becomes seemingly inevitable, like the workers' paradise in Marxian Communism.

An increasing consciousness of the limits of progress has destroyed the hope that it will become the means of bridging reality and fiction, of crossing the gap between the actual and the ideal. But the modern age is not alone in its unsusceptibility to the mythical *via media* of pro-

26. Frye, p. 326.

gress. Between the dissociation of myth from reality and
the emergence of the myth of progress lies a period in the
history of consciousness which produced Thomas More's
*Utopia.* The Tudor conception of history was cyclical, and
the constants of this cycle were man and God.

> But historical precedent as embodied in common law
> was only one part of a much greater whole, as Machia-
> velli pointed out. Implicit in the belief in the usefulness
> of history is the belief that history does repeat itself. . . .
> To Tudor England the reason for the repetition of
> historical patterns was to be found not only in the same-
> ness of man, but also in the persistent oneness of God.[27]

This conception of history presents two important facts
for the interpreter of *Utopia.* In an age no longer believing
in the reality of certain myths, most particularly the classical social myths, but not yet enamored of the myth of progress, mediating between reality and the utopian ideal is
a function neither of faith nor of physical ingenuity but
rather of the conscience and the consciousness of the environment of that conscience. Secondly, an age guided
in its historical perceptions by a cyclical theory, which sees
events rotating around the enduring sameness of man and
God, is bound to be sensitive to the movement of life about
the stationary rocks of man's nature and God's provident
judgment. These two ideas—the cyclical theory and the
awareness of utopia as myth—form a conceptual system
which launches the poet's mediating consciousness-in-
conscience into a dialogue between enduring human values
and the cyclical patterns of life. The dialogue to which

27. Lily B. Campbell, "Tudor Conceptions of History and Tragedy
in *A Mirrour for Magistrates,*" a Faculty Research Lecture at the University of California (Berkeley, Calif., 1936), p. 4.

More now turns—Book I—becomes an effort to place Hythlodaeus' Utopian idealism (or what Berger calls the "green world") into the context of this conceptual guide:

> The green world seems to possess two essential qualities: first, since it is only metaphorically a place or space, it embodies a condition whose value should not remain fixed, but should rather change according to the temporal process of which it is a part. It appears first as exemplary or appealing and lures us away from the evil or confusion of everyday life. But when it has fulfilled its moral, esthetic, social, cognitive or experimental functions, it becomes inadequate and its creator turns us out. Those who wish to remain, who cannot or will not be discharged, are presented as in some way deficient. Thus the second quality of the green world is that it is ambiguous: its usefulness and dangers arise from the same source. In its positive aspects it provides a temporary haven for recreation or clarification, experiment or relief; in its negative aspects it projects the urge of the paralyzed will to give up, escape, work magic, abolish time and flux and the intrusive reality of other minds.[28]

The first phase of *Utopia*—the letters of More to Peter Giles—establishes this ambiguous quality of the utopian myth: the ideal may exist but only in the mind and only temporarily. The mediating poet must not only accompany the visionary to Utopia but also must return to the real world. The question of why More limited his audience, excluding common folk and rulers alike while admitting only the most learned, can now be answered. The poet can mediate between the ideal world and the real world only

28. Berger, pp. 73–74.

for those who, like himself, can understand life as both pure and corrupt, who, like himself, have struggled to the consciousness-in-conscience both of the self (the essential) and of the external (the existential). Thus, the crucial interpretative suggestion which More supplies in his letters to Giles is that Utopia is merely a negative statement when considered alone; without an existential content Utopian idealism is an emasculating illusion. One must accompany the poet, not the philosopher, to Utopia, for the philosopher will seek to remain in his Nowhere of the mind, while the journey to Utopia only becomes meaningful when one returns—as only the poet can—to life. The ironic paradox of utopianism—the destruction of the individual in attaining the institutional ideal—is resolved only by the poet who fully understands the demands of both ideality and reality and comprehends them in a considered adjustment to this irony of the human situation.

The first phase of *Utopia* (the parerga), then, has translated a dilemma More acutely sensed into a semantic and artistic structure which he could communicate to his fellow humanists. More has projected two sets of problems. On the one hand, man is constantly seeking a better world, a new Eden, a utopia. On the other hand, man must constantly remind himself of the bonds which shackle him in everyday life. Somehow man must reconcile his idealism with his individualism, his hopes with his limitations. Through his introductory letters More has defined the parameters of this dilemma. The second or intermediate phase of *Utopia* confronts the dangers utopianism holds for man as an individual. Therefore, the dialogues of Book I are about the human personality's struggle to preserve its strengths in the face of an attractive, self-deceiving idealism. The third phase of *Utopia* (the monologic Book II) takes the reader to the ideal world itself. By showing him every part of Hythlodaeus' prefect island state, More invites the reader to ask how this dream world relates to the real world to which he must return at the end of Raphael's tale. The next chapter will deal with the ambiguity of the Utopian myth in its effects on those who journey to this illusory island; the third chapter will discuss the ambiguous lessons Utopia holds for life itself.

# 2

## Utopia, Book I: Defining the
## Self's Consciousness-in-Conscience
## through Dialogue

What I am calling the second phase of *Utopia*—Book I
—is based on two dialogues. The first, a framing "Dialogue of Counsel," deals with the responsibilities of a
learned person to respond to the call to counsel and the
manner in which he should respond.[1] Within this dialogue
on counselling is set a reported dialogue—Raphael's version of a debate which takes place at Cardinal Morton's
table after dinner. This "dialogue-within-a-dialogue" contrasts Hythlodaeus' philosophic perspective with the pragmatic political stance of the Cardinal. Though actually
written by More after Hythlodaeus' narrative (Book II),
these dialogues form the necessary preface to Raphael's
description of Utopia because they delineate the effect of
the utopian myth upon him. Beyond this, however, More
wrestles with a more subtle problem in these dialogues; he
not only reveals the self-consuming idealism of the narrator-guide but also attempts to define the proper relationship between idealism and the idealist. These two avenues
of discussion necessitate the dialogic structure of Book I.
Indeed, this dialogic format prefigures More's eventual
solution to the latter problem, a solution which he couches
in the metaphor of a play. Both the play metaphor and
the dialogic structure of Book I illustrate that More finds

1. The relation of the "Dialogue of Counsel" to More's personal
problems in the period when *Utopia* was written is discussed in Hexter,
*Utopia: The Biography*, pp. 98–155.

the proper relationship between one's life and one's hopes not in a final stance but in a method or perspective—the view which can look both out upon one's position in the world and in upon the philosophic realms of the mind. More's resolution of the dilemma for the individual in a utopian scheme lies in the detachment within involvement which is reflected in the attitudes of the dialogician and of the actor on the stage of the world.

The Dialogue of Counsel—the debate waged among Hythlodaeus, More, and Peter Giles about the social ills of contemporary society and the means of effecting reform through counsel—introduces both the issues and the characters of *Utopia* as a whole. Thomas More begins this dialogue by establishing a sense of verisimilitude through a series of portraits. First he presents the "peerless Cuthbert Tunstall" (47). Next comes Georges de Themsecke, "a man not only trained in eloquence but a natural orator—most learned, too, in the law and consummately skillful in diplomacy by native ability as well as by long experience" (47). A significant aspect of this portrait is the proper balance between native ability and knowledge gained by experience and education. The mediating factor between human potential and acquired knowledge, the special attribute of man which will prove to be a means of spanning so many disparate realms in *Utopia,* is his reason.

Man has always considered himself as a human being separate and distinct from and superior to the animal. He has therefore insisted that he should be considered as different; and that the difference consists in the assignment to himself of that reason which is denied to the animal world.[2]

2. James Brown Scott, *The Spanish Origin of International Law: Francisco de Vitoria and His Law of Nations* (Oxford, 1934), p. 165.

The conjunction of the discipline of learning and experience with man's rational faculty, as seen in the portrait of Themsecke, is the true source of human excellence.[3] Next, Thomas More introduces Peter Giles,

> a native of Antwerp, an honorable man of high position in his home town yet worthy of the very highest position, being a young man distinguished equally by learning and character; for he is most virtuous and most cultured, to all most courteous, but to his friends so open-hearted, affectionate, loyal, and sincere that you can hardly find one or two anywhere to compare with him as the perfect friend on every score. His modesty is uncommon; no one is less given to deceit, and none has a wiser simplicity of nature. (49)

The most detailed of the introductory portraits, the description of Peter Giles focuses on the key values of the humanist. The essence of his character lies in his wise simplicity, a quality apparently dependent upon his modesty, his open-hearted affection for friends, and his learn-

3. The union of learning and experience is approved by many humanists because it translates the excellence inherent in human nature into social activity: "the ever-recurring leitmotifs in the humanistic philosophy of life were the superiority of the *vita activa* over 'selfish' withdrawal into scholarship and contemplation . . . and the argument that the perfect life is not that of the 'sage,' but that of the citizen who, in addition to his studies, consummates his humanitas by shouldering man's social duties, and by serving his fellow-citizens in public office" (*Utopia*, p. 311, quoting H. Baron, *The Crisis of the Early Italian Renaissance, 1* [Princeton, 1955], p. 7. Baron has issued a revised, one volume edition of this book, Princeton, 1966). Strictly speaking, it is largely in quattrocento Florence that this aspiration to the vita activa took the form of political service. But it cannot be denied that the humanist program embodied a desire to affect man's conduct as well as his thought, a desire which, perhaps, reflects the quickening pace of life in the fifteenth and sixteenth centuries.

ing. Immediately following these portraits the dialogue begins; the reader is implicitly directed to apply the standard of values which they have established to the picture of Raphael Hythlodaeus as it now emerges. The first important detail of the portrait of the narrator is that his name is Raphael Hythlodaeus, for contained in this name is an ambiguity which shadows his every word. In his commentary Surtz suggests that " 'Hythlodaeus' means 'expert in trifles' or 'well-learned in nonsense.' "[4] Though "Raphael" may have no specific reference, it "is interpreted as 'God hath healed,' or 'the healing of God,' or 'the physician of health.' "[5]

The voyager Raphael Hythlodaeus becomes, then, both "the bringer of health" and "the teller of trifling tales." Thus, the ambiguity contained in the approach to life personified in Raphael Hythlodaeus begins with his name; one cannot be certain that he knows the difference between the truths he may bring and the trifling baggage which accompanies them. Only as he enters into a dialogue with the other characters of *Utopia* may the impact of his learning and experience upon his character as a human being be evaluated.

Peter Giles initiates this dialogue by asking Hythlodaeus why he has not entered the service of some king. "Thus, you would not only serve your own interests excellently but be of great assistance in the advancement of all your relatives and friends" (55). Hythlodaeus replies by arguing that he already has discharged his duty to them.

> "The possessions, which other men do not resign unless they are old and sick and even then resign unwillingly when incapable of retention, I divided among my rela-

4. *Utopia,* p. 301.
5. Ibid., p. 301.

tives and friends when I was not merely hale and hearty but actually young. I think they ought to be satisfied with this generosity from me and not to require or expect additionally that I should, for their sakes, enter into servitude to kings." (55)

This answer reveals several important components of Hythlodaeus' character. In the first place, he tends to measure the relations between men by an economic standard. Such a measure proves very convenient for him, since he can easily fulfill economic obligations. Indeed, one might suggest that he meets them all too easily, for physical possessions mean very little to him. By imposing an economic standard he is able to achieve what he really desires—psychological and philosophic detachment from his past. Without any deeper commitments, he is able to uproot himself and transplant himself into another context. Secondly, his unwillingness to "enter into servitude" reveals that the context in which he intends to take root will be of his own choosing. He thus takes the Renaissance hope for man—to be "the free and proud shaper of [his] own being"[6]—to its logical conclusion: philosophic man free of all traditional bonds.

Giles, understandably dissatisfied with Hythlodaeus' answer, presses Raphael further:

"But my conviction is," continued Peter, "whatever name you give to this mode of life, that it is the very way by which you can not only profit people both as private individuals and as members of the commonwealth but also render your own condition more prosperous." (55)

6. Giovanni Pico della Mirandola, *Oration on the Dignity of Man,* tr. A. Robert Caponigri (Chicago, 1956), p. 7.

To this Hythlodaeus answers that service implies a compromise not only of his independence but also of his integrity. To him, counselling means that he must "court the friendship of the great," an act which his "soul abhors" (57).

At this point the fictional More enters the dialogue and presents an argument which, it seems fair to conclude, the real More found quite persuasive:

> "But it seems to me you will do what is worthy of you and of this generous and truly philosophic spirit of yours if you so order your life as to apply your talent and industry to the public interest, even if it involves some personal disadvantages to yourself. This you can never do with as great profit as if you are a councilor to some great monarch and make him follow, as I am sure you will, straightforward and honorable courses. From the monarch, as from a never-failing spring, flows a stream of all that is good or evil over the whole nation." (57)

This argument opens several avenues of exchange. In the first place, one needs to understand properly the nature of counselling to come to terms with this position. Raphael begins to examine the issue when he initiates a discussion of the preoccupation with war, rather than peace, in most councils of kings. Then, in an argument which, in this context, can only be a red herring, he mentions sycophancy in king's courts. Though it is possible that Hythlodaeus fears that the flattery of the court may entice him from the truth, the self-confidence he displays on other occasions suggests that this objection is not meant as a serious argument. Rather, it serves merely as a transition into a long digression on the social ills of sixteenth-century

England. This "dialogue-within-a-dialogue," set at Cardinal Morton's table, is very important, and I shall return to it later. In the developing debate over the *personal* responsibility of a qualified person to enter the king's council, however, the discussion before Cardinal Morton is only an interruption.

After he finishes narrating the events at Cardinal Morton's, Raphael apologizes for his digression, and More returns the discussion to the nature of counselling in a sixteenth-century prince's court. One must not only weigh the possibility of affecting policy but also consider the inconvenience involved in accepting personal disadvantages for the good of the commonwealth. This position actually centers on the feelings of a citizen—and one wonders whether Raphael, in any philosophic or psychological sense, could be considered a citizen of any state. Finally, and most basically, the argument raised by More focuses upon the framing and purpose of an individual's life. The concept which More accepts as axiomatic Hythlodaeus not only rejects but cannot understand:

> "But it seems to me you will do what is worthy of you and of this generous and truly philosophic spirit of yours if you so order your life as to apply your talent and industry to the public interest, even if it involves some personal disadvantages to yourself." (57)

In this principle of ordering one's life so as to compensate in the mind for the disadvantages encountered in serving a cause outside of and greater than one's own being and happiness lies the key counter-statement to Raphael's ideal. Hythlodaeus would wish a state where rendering service to the community was coincident with realizing his own interests. In equating his own desires with those of the state, he fails to recognize that this means either being the only person in the state or coercing all other opinions into congruence with his own. More argues here that such a simplification makes life meaningless by destroying the complexity which characterizes the human species. Rather, he says, each should look to his own conscience, the province which is truly his to rule, and there attempt to institute his idealism; there and there alone can man determine the priorities of his allegiance, for only over his own life may he legitimately exercise his will. It is this discipline, this consciousness-in-conscience, which ultimately separates More from Hythlodaeus not only on the question of counsel but on every aspect of self-definition in *Utopia.*

Beyond this general principle of ordering one's life, however, More raises several specific questions about the nature of counselling in the courts of contemporary Europe. Hythlodaeus replies by giving two examples. The first example is that of the French court:

> "Come now, suppose I were at the court of the French king and sitting in his privy council. In a most secret meeting, a circle of his most astute councilors over which he personally presides is setting its wits to work to consider by what crafty machinations he may keep his hold on Milan and bring back into his power the Naples which has been eluding his grasp; then overwhelm Venice and subjugate the whole of Italy; next bring under his sway Flanders, Brabant, and, finally, the whole of Burgundy—and other nations, too, whose territory he has already conceived the idea of usurping."
> (87)

The satire at this point becomes very rich. One councilor proposes a temporary treaty with Venice "just as long as

the king will find it convenient" (87). Such treaties of
convenience were very common at that time, and Venice
had been shuttled back and forth according to the ambi-
tions of Louis XII and Pope Julius II less than five years
before this passage was written. Other suggestions—such
as the hiring of German *Landsknechte,* bargains with Ferdinand involving transfers of land as well as the prospect of
a marriage alliance, and the idea of fostering a false
claimant to the English throne (89)—find a similar source
in the turmoil and intrigue of the period.[7] The thrust of
the satire reveals the duplicity rampant in European affairs. But Hythlodaeus' response also suggests a deeper
problem:

> "In such a meeting, I say, when such efforts are being
> made, when so many distinguished persons are vying
> with each other in proposals of a warlike nature, what
> if an insignificant fellow like myself were to get up and
> advise going on another tack? Suppose I expressed the
> opinion that Italy should be left alone. Suppose I argued
> that we should stay at home because the single kingdom
> of France by itself was almost too large to be governed
> well by a single man so that the king should not dream of
> adding other dominions under his sway." (89)

What Hythlodaeus is pointing to is not simple duplicity:
the judgment of these councilors has been corrupted
from within. They believe that the king, as the embodi-
ment of France's hopes and destiny, has a natural right
to pursue these schemes—that their counsels frame the
policies which follow naturally from France's greatness.

---

7. See Surtz's Commentary to these pages: *Utopia,* pp. 350–59.

If France, for example, decided upon conquering Milan and Naples or the whole of Italy, no other prince would have offered a French statesman the smallest sum of money for executing such a plan. They would gladly have paid them the greatest bribes for abandoning their schemes, if it had not been impossible even for the most influential minister to oppose measures which the king and the nation regarded as conducive to the greatness for which, they thought, they were predestined.[8]

Thus, what Hythlodaeus is arguing in reply to More is not that he would be unable to turn back the counsels of sycophants but that many councilors, citizens, and even the king himself, believe these corrupt arguments and put them forth in good faith because they are ingrained in their political thinking. Such men and such beliefs, Raphael concludes, would be impervious to his recommendations.

More's response to Hythlodaeus throws into naked relief one difference between the two men. More argues that Hythlodaeus has no conception of philosophy within the context of a given state:

"In the private conversation of close friends this academic philosophy is not without its charm, but in the councils of kings, where great matters are debated with great authority, there is no room for these notions."

"That is just what I meant," he rejoined, "by saying there is no room for philosophy with rulers."

"Right," I declared, "that is true—not for this academic philosophy which thinks that everything is suitable to every place. But there is another philosophy,

8. *Calendar of Letters, Despatches, and State Papers . . . Between England and Spain, Preserved . . . at Simancas and Elsewhere,* Vol. 2: *Henry VIII: 1509–1524,* ed. G. A. Bergenroth (London, 1886), p. xxi.

more practical for statesmen, which knows its stage, adapts itself to the play in hand, and performs its role neatly and appropriately." (99)

The philosophic community has no room for political compromise, nor can it tolerate or even recognize the integrity of positions different from its own. Hythlodaeus has, in effect, resigned his membership in any community, just as he has resigned his membership in his family. "If I would stick to the truth, I must needs speak in the manner I have described" (101). Raphael is blinded by the truths of his own vision. Not only has his philosophic insight alienated him from a sense of community, divorced him from all normal social ties, and eradicated his natural regard for his fellow human beings; it has also barred him from a proper understanding of himself as a man and has made him belligerent for a cause to the point of losing sight of the very people who give that cause meaning. "Whatever play is being performed, perform it as best you can, and do not upset it all simply because you think of another which has more interest," More says (99).[9] Hythlodaeus has taken to himself the horrible burden of

9. The image of life as a play is a familiar one in humanist writings (for some references to its use, see *Utopia*, p. 372). Often the lesson of this play metaphor is that wisdom should be governed by prudence (cf. Erasmus, *The Praise of Folly*, tr. H. H. Hudson [New York, 1941], pp. 37–38). A striking application of this metaphor to the drama of the political world may be found in More's *Richard III (Yale Edition of the Complete Works of St. Thomas More*, Vol. 2: *The History of King Richard III* [New Haven, 1965], pp. 80–81). As the editor of this volume, Richard Sylvester, notes: "The kings' games, played upon scaffolds are the public consequences of tyranny and More was always a player, detached in his role, but constantly striving to act his part to the best of his ability. As one critic has finely said, in commenting on this scene in the *Richard*, More 'acknowledges the difficulties of living under a tyranny at the same time that he urges his readers to act like rational men and oppose it' " (p. cii, quoting Dean, "Literary Problems,"

absolute truth. Such is the danger of the utopian *telos* myth—to transmute everything into the ideal, "to kill the organism in order to control it, to combat that ceaseless process of self-transformation which lies at the very origin of species."[10] By assuming such a role Hythlodaeus, paradoxically, loses his chance to become a free citizen in a human community: either he must control the state or he must be crushed by it. This dichotomy is the end result of his insistence on complete independence.

The very form of More's argument—his use of the theatrical metaphor—embodies the most complete difference between the two men. Raphael is controlled, one might almost say consumed, by his utopian ideal. The conception of life as a play reveals a contrasting viewpoint—a detachment in involvement which can be discerned in every facet of More's life. More's central position—"so order your life as to apply your talent and industry to the public interest, even if it involves some personal disadvantages to yourself" (57)—is one to which Raphael cannot reply because he does not understand what More means by ordering one's life for the purpose of serving the public interest:

> "As to that indirect approach of yours, I cannot see its relevancy; I mean your advice to use my endeavors, if all things cannot be made good, at least to handle them tactfully and, as far as one may, to make them as little bad as possible." (103)

---

p. 35). Thus, though More opposes tyranny and would agree with many of Hythlodaeus' indictments of contemporary practices in Europe, he would have the reader understand that Raphael's insights must be supplemented by recognition of the reality of the shackles which current abuses place upon reforming zeal and ideal solutions.

10. Mumford, "Utopia," p. 275.

How far Hythlodaeus is from understanding this point of view is revealed by his attempts to refute it. In the first place, he misconstrues tact as dissembling. Secondly, he overlooks the consciousness-in-conscience involved by suggesting that More's method will either seduce him from truth or manipulate him as a screen to hide the wickedness of others (101). More's own life (and death) testifies to his impregnability to these two threats. Finally, as may be seen in the anecdote Hythlodaeus draws from Plato (103), he completely fails to perceive man's communal nature, the sense of brotherhood which should pervade the human community. Thus, as the dialogue of Book I draws to a close, the reader should be struck by the contrast in personalities and understandings which has emerged. On the one hand there is Hythlodaeus, consumed by his utopian ideal, acute in his satire on contemporary Europe, but immune to any self-awareness or recognition of his membership in any community, whether it be family, friends, or state. On the other hand there is More, sensitive to and qualifying Hythlodaeus' utopian ideals through consciousness-in-conscience and recognition of his traditional, human, and communal inheritance.

If More finds Hythlodaeus uncompromising in his attitudes toward counselling, however, he also finds his "generous and truly philosophic spirit" (57) and his learning and experience highly commendable. Though Raphael's independence of spirit stops short of the proper mixture of the contemplative *and* active ideals, his philosophic insights raise him above the dreary calculations of the average councilor. To understand fully where More and Hythlodaeus part company requires a recognition of the paths they travel together. Thus, we should return and fill out the lines of the portrait of Hythlodaeus suggestively developed before the dialogue begins to focus upon the differences between Raphael Hythlodaeus and Thomas More.

The first of Hythlodaeus' engaging traits is a mysterious and undeniably romantic strangeness. More first sees Raphael from a distance, locked in conversation with Peter Giles.

> Mass being over, I was about to return to my lodging when I happened to see him in conversation with a stranger, a man of advanced years, with sunburnt countenance and long beard and cloak hanging carelessly from his shoulder, while his appearance and dress seemed to me to be those of a ship's captain. (49)

This portrait develops two tantalizing images. On the one hand there is Hythlodaeus the seaman. The alienation of the voyager reflects the ultimate dependence of Hythlodaeus' views on peripheral isolation. But the voyager in an age of exploration still alive to the suggestive example of Mandeville represents as well an ideal of independence which is obviously attractive. To be totally free offers an individual the opportunity to be as he would like to be.[11] This freedom is expanded in the other suggestive details of the portrait. The beard, the sunburned countenance, the cloak hung carelessly from the shoulder, the name "Raphael," all suggest the image of a hermit or prophet. Thus Raphael also stands in the long line of Old Testament prophets bearing a message to beleaguered and corrupted man. He represents a creative thrust of the self-shaping aspirations of humanity, a thrust embodied in two attractive and traditional images of independent quest for truth —the voyager and the prophet. His insights, however disengaged from reality, operate as emblems of an enduring psychological and dramatic appeal.

11. Berger, "The Renaissance Imagination," p. 69.

Further details of Hythlodaeus' portrait before his actual appearance in the dialogue enhance these suggestions. His voyage represents a mythological and philosophic exploration, as is suggested by Giles' comparison of him to Ulysses and Plato (49). Moreover, the name "Raphael"

> might suggest Hythlodaeus' role of salvation-bringer to Christian Europe. Pico in "De dignitate hominis," exhorts his readers: "Let us summon Raphael, the heavenly physician, to free us with ethics and dialectics as with health-bringing medicines" *(Opera, I,* Basel, 1572–73, 321).[12]

Not only does this name reinforce the prophetic suggestions; the image of the prophet is integrated into the image of the physician. Hythlodaeus' dramatic appeal as physician of Europe becomes explicit toward the end of the dialogue:

> "By this type of legislation, I maintain, as sick bodies which are past cure can be kept up by repeated medical treatments, so these evils, too, can be alleviated and made less acute. There is no hope, however, of a cure and a return to a healthy condition as long as each individual is master of his own property." (105)

The detached voyager, the prophet of doom and necessary violent reform, the metaphysical doctor—all of these figures suggest the radicalism of Hythlodaeus' philosophy. The comparisons with Vespucci and with the contemplative hermit ("These two sayings are constantly on his lips: 'He who has no grave is covered by the sky,' and 'From all places it is the same distance to heaven' " [51])

12. *Utopia,* p. 302.

express the mythical and romantic attractiveness of the man. Thus, though the development of his character in the dialogue alerts the reader to the critical weaknesses of Hythlodaeus' character, it cannot eliminate the drama, the attractiveness, the romantic idealism which is his other dimension.

The engaging qualities of Hythlodaeus find expression in the acuity of perception which his disaffection from reality allows him. Though his refusal of the active life ends in misdirected enthusiasm, his contemplative isolation channels his critical perceptions to the very heart of many social problems. His criticism, when directed to contemporary patterns of behavior, is incisive and finds More largely in agreement. Hythlodaeus unfolds his scathing wit most clearly in the tale of the Anemolian ambassadors:

Consequently the three ambassadors made a grand entry with a suite of a hundred followers, all in parti-colored clothes and most in silk. The ambassadors themselves, being noblemen at home, were arrayed in cloth of gold, with heavy gold necklaces and earrings, with gold rings on their fingers, and with strings of pearls and gems upon their caps; in fact, they were decked out with all those articles which in Utopia are used to punish slaves, to stigmatize evil-doers, or to amuse children. It was a sight worth seeing to behold their cockiness when they compared their grand clothing with that of the Utopians, who had poured out into the street to see them pass. On the other hand, it was no less delightful to notice how much they were mistaken in their sanguine expectations and how far they were from obtaining the consideration which they had hoped to get. To the eyes of all the Utopians, with the exception of the very few who for a good reason had visited foreign countries, all this gay show appeared disgraceful. They therefore bowed to the lowest of the party as to the masters but took the ambassadors themselves to be slaves because they were wearing gold chains, and passed them over without any deference whatever. (155)

By contrasting different customs Hythlodaeus not only parodies the vanity of the European nobility but also reveals how far the false distinctions of men may vary from true worth.

The Utopians wonder that any mortal takes pleasure in the uncertain sparkle of a tiny jewel or precious stone when he can look at a star or even the sun itself. They wonder that anyone can be so mad as to think himself more noble on account of the texture of a finer wool, since, however fine the texture is, a sheep once wore the wool and yet all the time was nothing more than a sheep. (157)

Europeans attempt to perpetuate exploitation by constructing false hierarchies. They invert nature and make scarcity rather than true worth or accessibility the measure of value. The Utopian treatment of the ambassadors as slaves is profoundly accurate: Europeans have made themselves slaves to gold and precious gems. Though values are man-made, they are falsely made when constructed on principles not in conformity with nature's benevolence.

Moreover, the foundations man has made for judgments of value enslave him in a deeper sense. They create a substitute providence, a fortune which may operate capriciously rather than a fortune which reflects the natural benignity of Divine Providence. In other words, by judging men's fortunes in materialistic rather than spiritual terms, the Europeans make man subject to the mutabilities of the physical world rather than the ennobled instrument of spiritual constancy:

> This is true to such an extent that a blockhead who has no more intelligence than a log and who is as dishonest as he is foolish keeps in bondage many wise men and good men merely for the reason that a great heap of gold coins happens to be his. Yet if some chance or some legal trick (which is as apt as chance to confound high and low) transfers it from this master to the lowest rascal in his entire household, he will surely very soon pass into the service of his former servant—as if he were a mere appendage of and addition to the coins! (157)

Man has the freedom to choose his own rulers, and it is the false and perverse choice of the Europeans which subjugates them to a seemingly inexplicable, capricious fortune rather than to a perhaps inscrutable but undeniably just Providence.

Thus, Hythlodaeus' alienation enables him to see a fact with which More agrees and which he wishes to make the reader see: to a large extent man does shape his own destiny and does so most beneficially when he properly understands his nature and properly employs his reason. When Hythlodaeus concentrates his dramatic power on this insight he becomes a truly attractive figure to More and the reader. But when the time comes to make the choice between destinies, Hythlodaeus' enthusiasm for the Utopian ideal begins to fog his vision. To the extent that he remains sensitive to man's personally creative means—his reason, the family, respected authority, awareness of his position in the universe as well as in the community of men—to that extent does he earn the reader's and More's approval. But Hythlodaeus' commitment to the Utopian ideal as a system finally leads to a poorly chosen *means.* The danger is implicit in the demands made by a model, for the greatest strength of a model is its ability, through its command of all social forces, to preserve itself intact. This quality becomes explicit in Busleyden's letter to More prefaced to *Utopia:*

> Such notable disasters, devastations, destructions, and calamities of war our commonwealths one and all will easily escape provided that they organize themselves exactly on the one pattern of the Utopian commonwealth and do not depart from it, as they say, by a hair's breadth. (37)

Reflected in the "ease" of this undeviating agreement with the Utopian norm is the danger of idealism—the smooth and simplified result is often the product of coercing all persons into impotent submission. The same loss of self occurs when Hythlodaeus subsumes his entire personality in his idealism—he becomes unconscious of his humanity, and his individual expression is numbed by the sterile rationalism of his effective and efficient utopianism.

One can see from this that the dialogue between the fictional More and Hythlodaeus brought before the reader by the mediating poet is rather complex. Raphael's alienation, the fact that he has made the trip to Utopia, is of immense creative importance. He engages the reader and More in the utopian *telos.* He has brought the ideal before the mind. But, in doing so, he has lost his place, his citizenship, his membership in the human community. He belongs to the contemplative ideal he has seen; he belongs to the Nowhere of the mind. It is left to More and the reader to return from Utopia, to relocate themselves in the

European community and to joust with life. Hythlodaeus has given the mind the script, the scripture; More and the reader must act out the play, realize the word. The ideal rules only in the mythical, paradisal garden; More and the reader must return to life's real, not romantic, dream, must reassimilate themselves into that world of inextricably mixed good and evil that is man's patrimony.

Just as More adjusts the reader's response to Hythlodaeus in the Dialogue of Counsel by personifying points of view in the characters, so, too, does he orient the reader in the dialogue-within-a-dialogue by using portraits as emblems of the different political perspectives discussed. One point of reference in this satiric kaleidoscope is "the Right Reverend Father, John Cardinal Morton, Archbishop of Canterbury, and then also Lord Chancellor of England" (59).[13] Morton exemplifies the important characteristics of a prominent man in public affairs:

"He was a man, my dear Peter (for More knows about him and needs no information from me), who deserved respect as much for his prudence and virtue as for his authority. . . . His countenance inspired respect rather than fear. In conversation he was agreeable, though serious and dignified. Of those who made suit to him he

13. Morton's symbolic role may partially be understood by considering his relation to another of More's literary efforts of this period—his *History of King Richard III*. " 'Wise men' like Cardinal Morton, who figures in both the *History* and the *Utopia,* had removed Richard from the throne and had passed on the story of his reign to Thomas More. Their 'wisdom' was practical, expedient, efficient; it met tyranny on its own terms and bested it in the world of action" (Sylvester, *Richard,* p. cii). Thus, Cardinal Morton personifies man's efforts to fight against tyranny completely within the context of political reality; he represents that political acumen which must supplement idealism if a good commonwealth is ever to be achieved.

enjoyed making trial by rough address, but in a harmless way, to see what mettle and what presence of mind a person would manifest. . . . His speech was polished and pointed. His knowledge of law was profound, his ability incomparable, and his memory astonishingly retentive, for he had improved his extraordinary natural qualities by learning and practice. . . . by many and great dangers he had acquired a statesman's sagacity which, when thus learned, is not easily forgotten." (59–61)

Because Morton's character has been forged in the hot fire of politics he knows the often overpowering demands of reality. "He knows better than to hope by his reason, rather than by his status, to influence or improve the human specimens at his table."[14] While Hythlodaeus bars reality from his realm of philosophic reason, Morton tends to bar reason from the political arena. The Cardinal is intrigued by rational theories but will introduce them into reality only experimentally (81). Thus, while the Dialogue of Counsel focused upon the necessity to preserve a sense of commitment to political activity within the framework of an enlightened idealism, this dialogue, set at Cardinal Morton's table, centers upon the need to balance dreams with an awareness of the limitations of the human personality. In both cases the thrust of More's analysis is toward the relationship of the individual reformer to his ideals. In both cases More resolves this problem by projecting into the dialogue his search for a link between the immediacy of involvement and the remoteness of detached reflection.

This discussion between Cardinal Morton and Hythlodaeus is introduced and controlled by their contrasting

14. Berger, p. 65.

perspectives on the problem of reform. Raphael represents the theoretical man, the rational planner; Morton stands as the symbol of the practical man, the politician. Raphael's antagonist in this satiric dialogue is a simple "layman, learned in the laws of [his] country" (61). He possesses neither the political nature of Morton nor the independent philosophic nature of Raphael. This lawyer is the emblem of a third position, which is to be lampooned. He epitomizes the abuse of the law in England which has corrupted the theoretical ideal man of common law—"the free and lawful man. . .honest in his dealings, efficient in his work."[15]

Hythlodaeus sets the theoretical tone of this dialogue-within-a-dialogue by revealing how the lawyer's law has departed from its ideal.

"Theft alone is not a grave offense that ought to be punished with death, and no penalty that can be devised is sufficient to restrain from acts of robbery those who have no other means of getting a livelihood. In this respect not your country alone but a great part of our world resembles bad schoolmasters, who would rather beat than teach their scholars. You ordain grievous and terrible punishments for a thief when it would have been much better to provide some means of getting a living, that no one should be under this terrible necessity first of stealing and then of dying for it." (61)

Hythlodaeus' attack on this lawyer's conception of the law is two-pronged. On the one hand, the law is too harsh, establishing penalties that far exceed the iniquity of the crime. On the other hand, and more importantly, the law

15. Richard O'Sullivan, K.C., "Social Theories of St. Thomas More," *Dublin Review, 199* (July to September 1936), 52.

has perverted its proper relationship to man: it should, like
a good schoolmaster, enhance man's natural virtues by en-
couraging an "acquisition" of appropriate skills and attitudes. Learning and the law, properly conceived, are both
instruments intended to supplement human nature and to
become the true sources of human excellence.

The lawyer first attempts to rebut this line of attack by
arguing that every reasonable effort has been made to
cooperate with man's natural capacities.

'We have,' said the fellow, 'made sufficient provision
for this situation. There are manual crafts. There is
farming. They might maintain themselves by these pur-
suits if they did not voluntarily prefer to be rascals.' (61)

In essence the lawyer is arguing that the opportunities for
a wide diffusion of land and employment are offered
through the law, and that only laziness or obstinacy pre-
vents men from taking advantage of it. This argument
leads to an investigation of all social forces in order to
determine whether their joint effect is to help or to hinder
man's potentialities. What really is at issue are those social
forces which deflect man's pursuit of his natural inclinations by attacking his conception of himself as a reasonable
and free individual.

The first perversion of this humanistic ideal is the
"noble" practice of keeping idle retainers, henchmen, and
other persons in impractical and useless capacities.

"Now there is the great number of noblemen who not
only live idle themselves like drones on the labor of
others, as for instance the tenants of their estates whom
they fleece to the utmost by increasing the returns (for
that is the only economy they know of, being otherwise
so extravagant as to bring themselves to beggary!) but

who also carry about with them a huge crowd of idle attendants who have never learned a trade for a livelihood. As soon as their master dies or they themselves fall sick, these men are turned out at once, for the idle are maintained more readily than the sick, and often the heir is not able to support as large a household as his father did, at any rate at first." (63)

This passage does condemn the inequitable law which allows the rich to exploit the poor, but its main attack centers upon that social pattern which enfeebles self-reliance and freedom. The practice of keeping idle retainers and attendants eliminates man's liberty, makes him dependent upon others, in effect, fosters effeminate creatures unable to realize their full potentiality. By making people property, one overturns the conception of the ordinary man as free and replaces it with the idea of the depersonalized man —a mere cog in the human machine. By placing his reliance in property and position rather than in his own person, man becomes womanish and weak.

"The [farmers] know full well that a man who has been softly brought up in idleness and luxury and has been wont in sword and buckler to look down with a swaggering face on the whole neighborhood and to think himself far above everybody will hardly be fit to render honest service to a poor man with spade and hoe, for a scanty wage, and on frugal fare." (63)

The lawyer, in attempting to refute this criticism, reveals that he does not share the conception of human nature embodied in the law.

'But this,' the fellow retorted, 'is just the sort of man we ought to encourage most. On them, being men of a

loftier and nobler spirit than craftsmen and farmers,
depend the strength and sinews of our army when we
have to wage war.' (63)

The representative of English law becomes the physical
symbol of its most complete perversion. In place of a concept of man based on his reason, his essential honesty, his
industriousness, and his brotherhood with his fellows, he
puts an enfeebling doctrine based on false degree, power
and position, duplicity and exploitation. What he sees as
visible strength is really moral weakness.

The emasculation of the population by the "noble"
classes is a sickness which English society shares with the
rest of Europe. But the integrity of the English common
man, based on a continuous tradition of land ownership
and independence, is imperiled by a danger peculiar to
England—her sheep.

'Your sheep,' [Hythlodaeus] answered, 'which are
usually so tame and so cheaply fed, begin now, according to report, to be so greedy and wild that they devour
human beings themselves and devastate and depopulate
fields, houses, and towns.' (65–67)

In fact, this image of sheep "devouring" men coalesces with
the picture of the nobles "devouring" the personalities of
their attendants to reveal the source of this insidious corruption—greed. Not content with the profits earned from
the estates by their predecessors, these noblemen aspire to
raise ever more sheep, and for this they must enclose the
land. The enclosure movement, the result of this compact
of greed, uproots the local populations, severs ties stretch-
ing back over generations, and negates the social ideal of a
wide and plentiful distribution of property and work.

In doing so it takes a once stable, healthy population and casts them into a life of hopeless wandering.

"After they have soon spent that trifle in wandering from place to place, what remains for them but to steal and be hanged—justly, you may say!—or to wander and beg. And yet even in the latter case they are cast into prison as vagrants for going about idle when, though they most eagerly offer their labor, there is no one to hire them. For there is no farm work, to which they have been trained, to be had, when there is no land for plowing left. A single shepherd or herdsman is sufficient for grazing livestock on that land for whose cultivation many hands were once required to make it raise crops." (67)

The point of this satiric indictment is alienation. The ideal from which law and society have departed, the theory to which practice must return, sees man freely exercising his reason, employing his natural abilities and his property to supply his own wants and the needs of those dear to him, "living in a relation of friendship with his fellow men"[16] based upon his communal instincts as well as upon the familiarity of custom and acquaintance contained in a life close to the soil.

The theoretical aim of the legal reforms Hythlodaeus suggests is to reinstate the natural "honest "man, to restore him to useful cooperation with a benevolent and provident Mother Nature, and to resuscitate the "farmsteads" and family economy built around land and familiar trades.

"Cast out these ruinous plagues. Make laws that the destroyers of farmsteads and country villages should

16. O'Sullivan, p. 52.

either restore them or hand them over to people who
will restore them and who are ready to build. Restrict
this right of rich individuals to buy up everything and
this license to exercise a kind of monopoly for themselves. Let fewer be brought up in idleness. Let farming
be resumed and let cloth-working be restored once more
that there may be honest jobs to employ usefully that
idle throng, whether those whom hitherto pauperism
has made thieves or those who, now being vagrants or
lazy servants, in either case are likely to turn out
thieves." (69–71)[17]

Hythlodaeus' philosophic detachment has enabled him to
see into the very heart of European corruption, into the
irrational twisting of human nature contained in the in-
verted values and unnatural hierarchies of sixteenth-century society. His theoretical solution is rational, coherent,
integrated, effective, efficient; but it is also coercive and
decreed from above; it disrupts any sense of continuity
with tradition, and it is violent and unilateral reform. His
social theory overlooks reality; it rests upon fiat, not political compromise. The end he envisions allows no room for
either the individual or the traditional workings of society's

17. Some of the statutes which parallel Raphael's programs are suggested in the Commentary: "Bowden summarizes as follows: 'Between
1489 and 1597 eleven Acts of Parliament were passed having as their
object the prevention of depopulation. These Acts were not strictly
enforced, for their administration lay in the hands of those most opposed to them, and the government resorted to other measures with little
apparent success' *(Wool Trade,* p. 110)" *(Utopia,* p. 339). The ineffectiveness of this attempt to reform abuses through the promulgation
of rational laws justifies the rather uninterested hearing Cardinal
Morton gives to Raphael's proposal. It also points up the necessarily
complex interplay between ideality and reality, between institutional
reform and individual regeneration, which Hythlodaeus is constantly
trying to simplify in accordance with his rationally conceived social
theory.

corrective mechanisms. Therefore, Cardinal Morton enters the dialogue actively and introduces the knowledge
gleaned from years of political experience. He shifts the
grounds of the discussion from political theorizing to concrete programs.

"But now I am eager to have you tell me, my dear
Raphael, why you think that theft ought not to be
punished with the extreme penalty, or what other penalty you yourself would fix, which would be more bene-
ficial to the public. I am sure that not even you think it
ought to go unpunished. Even as it is, with death as the
penalty, men still rush into stealing. What force and
what fear, if they once were sure of their lives, could
deter the criminals? They would regard themselves as
much invited to crime by the mitigation of the penalty
as if a reward were offered." (71–73)

Morton's query is intended to lead to a discussion of immediate legal reforms. The Cardinal seems to regard all
such philosophizing, especially in the light of his own experience of its ineffectiveness, as essentially irrelevant to
the real world.

Morton humors Hythloday as he humors the lawyer,
friar and parasite—a Chaucerian gallery eminently
qualified to bring on an attack. He amuses himself with
them, is amused by them, allows them to vent their
vanities and theories at his table, and dismisses them
when it is time "to heare his sueters."[18]

Thus, Morton serves to call us back from the world of
theoretical coherence and idealism. Since he sees in cor-

18. Berger, p. 64.

rupted persons a split between ideality and reality similar to that in the law, he considers the chances of repairing the rift through rational laws alone very slim. At the same time, however, one must continue to recognize that the law is society's one defense against chaos and anarchy. Hythlodaeus responds to Morton's query by citing the example of the Polylerites, a nation "free and autonomous in its laws. They are far from the sea, almost ringed round by mountains, and altogether satisfied with the products of their own land" (75). Their isolation strongly recommends their example to philosophic interpretation.[19] Conveniently, the Polylerites are self-satisfied and nonmilitaristic, frown upon trading, and are geographically immune to assault from without, qualities few would hope to apply to England. Indeed, Hythlodaeus' Polylerite penal code is the perfect expression of the detached and rational reformer. In the first place, instead of fines or confiscation of stolen goods by the prince, the objects are returned, either in kind or in value, to the original owner. Moreover, punishment is equitable; thieves repay their debt to society by useful labor rather than with their lives (77). Finally, the Polylerites supplement the punitive dimensions of their criminal code with efforts to rehabilitate the convict (79).

Though this program of legal reform still is tinged with ideality and philosophic isolation, its concrete suggestions strike Cardinal Morton as potentially more immediately realizable than the vast reforms Hythlodaeus had proposed earlier. Therefore, Morton outlines an experimental implementation of the idea (81). What Cardinal Morton con-

---

19. Though the Polylerites are isolated, their distance from the rest of the world is a natural result of their geography (like Switzerland); it is not the planned discontinuity of the Utopians, where a fifteen-mile channel is dredged out to confirm physically their philosophic detachment (113).

cedes to Hythlodaeus in this experiment seems to be the minimum response possible to Raphael's suggestive idealism. Morton, schooled in the violently fluctuating world of court politics, focuses on the limitations inherent in the human personality and its traditional social context. Hythlodaeus, schooled in his remote Platonic academy, detaches himself from any tradition and from any consideration of man's wickedness. He brings forward a coherent social theory—a goal for human conduct. But Cardinal Morton strips away the impact of the theoretical aspects of this vision by pointing out that every program of reform must be initiated in the world of corrupted tradition. Morton's political sense neutralizes the appeal of Hythlodaeus' theorizing. Though the reader must penetrate beyond the political compromises of Morton's world, he cannot proceed all the way to Hythlodaeus' rationally coherent society. "Paradoxically, the ideal commonwealth, if it were to be realized at all, had to be born out of a society in which the seeds of tyranny were already well planted."[20] Thus, More has arrived at a fine but important compromise between the positions of Cardinal Morton and Raphael Hythlodaeus. From Morton he has drawn the lesson that all reform in European society must begin with a regeneration of the human character. But Morton sees this merely as a project of political juggling. Thomas More is searching for a much more fundamental level upon which to begin building the "best state of a commonwealth." Consequently, he is willing to be inspired by Raphael's suggestive idealism. More recognizes, however, that a utopian dream is of value only if the dreamer can remain free from its consuming effect upon his mind. To accomplish this he uses Morton's political sense to balance

20. Sylvester, *Richard III*, p. cii.

Hythlodaeus' philosophic vision, a balance creating a detached involvement, an awareness of all the forces and claims, both idealistic and realistic, bearing upon man.

But defining the proper relationship of the utopian dreamer to his dream is only half the task More has set for himself; he must also delineate the true content or meaning of the utopian myth. The key to this second project is to balance the visions of the prophet with the awareness of the politician. More poses this problem in the closing pages of the dialogues of Book I when Hythlodaeus proposes his most extreme and most rationally coherent ideal—the community of property of the Utopians. The contrast between Hythlodaeus' negative idealism (as embodied in his vast reforms totally divorced from a historical context) and More's tentative but distinctly positive approach to introducing ideals into life (as suggested in his conclusion that one must begin "with the play in hand") has been developing throughout Book I. It looks back to a reference made early in the book to the character of Raphael's exploring: " 'But you are quite mistaken,' said he [Giles], 'for his [Hythlodaeus'] sailing has not been like that of Palinurus but that of Ulysses or, rather, of Plato' " (49). More presents here a progression of three voyages. As Surtz notes, the reference to Palinurus should remind one of the traveler who fell asleep at the tiller and was lost to the sea.[21] The reader should understand that Raphael Hythlodaeus, unlike Palinurus, has been very alert in his travels. His journey was more like that of Ulysses, having taken him to many strange places; but it was most like that of Plato—a philosophic exploration. The role of the state in Plato's *Republic,* therefore, takes on great importance as a conceptual guide.

21. *Utopia,* p. 301.

Plato's state is a stage in examining the nature of true justice. As such, the state is one level of abstraction in a progression from the existential to the essential, from the real to the poetic and philosophic. To understand his Ideal State is really to understand its role as a link between the ideal and the accidental worlds.

But Plato is really arguing from his social model to the individual, not from the individual to society. The censorship of Homer and the other poets, for example, illustrates how the wise man uses literature, what he accepts and rejects of it in forming his own beliefs, rather than what society ought to do to literature.[22]

22. Frye, "Varieties of Literary Utopias," p. 332. Anemolius, the poet laureate of Utopia, draws an interesting comparison between his island commonwealth and Plato's republic: "The ancients called me Utopia or Nowhere because of my isolation. At present, however, I am a rival of Plato's republic, perhaps even a victor over it. The reason is that what he has delineated in words I alone have exhibited in men and resources and laws of surpassing excellence. Deservedly ought I to be called by the name of Eutopia or Happy Land" (21). What is interesting in this comparison is the emphasis upon the translation of the verbal ideal of Plato into an activated program, thus bridging the gap which Frye observes that Plato has created between word and deed: "We notice, however, that as early as the Fifth Book Socrates has begun to deprecate the question of the practicability of establishing his Republic, on the ground that thought is one thing and action another" (Frye, p. 331). The limitation of Plato's Ideal State to a mere image rather than a realizable form was noted by one of More's contemporaries as well: "Going further, Lupset sees Plato's republic as impossible for man's nature: 'Plato imagynyd only and dremyd apon such a commyn wele as neuer yet was found, nor neuer, I thynke, schalbe, except God wold send downe hys angellys, and of them make a cyte; for man by nature ys so frayle and corrupt, that so many wyse men in a commynalty to fynd, I thynke hyt playn impossybul' " (Utopia, p. 375, quoting Starkey, Dialogue, p. 163). Perhaps More, thinking over the disparity between word and action which Plato has forced upon himself in his Republic "by arguing from his social model to the individual," saw that by turning Plato around, by proceeding to a social

Thus, Plato's Ideal State is really a state of consciousness
—an effort to understand man's role in society without the
vocabulary and expertise of anthropology and social psy-
chology. Like Plato's Ideal State, the Utopian commonwealth described by Hythlodaeus may be meant to be seen
as a metaphor for the manner in which man mediates
between his fantasies and hopes and his human commitments. The problem then becomes how More intends the
reader to understand Utopian institutions. The Utopian
institution which poses the main problem of interpretation is, of course, community of property. The question
which must be asked is whether this communism should be
viewed as a formal institution or whether, like the Ideal
State in Plato's *Republic,* it is intended as a means of
analyzing the ideal personal consciousness-in-conscience
of true community.

The importance of Plato's *Republic* and his Ideal State
as conceptual references for Hythlodaeus' advocacy of
Utopia becomes even clearer when Raphael makes his
transition from the dialogues of Book I to his monologic
narrative in Book II, for the pivotal element in this transition is Plato:

> "As a result, when in my heart I ponder on the extreme-
> ly wise and holy institutions of the Utopians, among
> whom, with very few laws, affairs are ordered so aptly

---

ideal through the reform of man's nature, "so frayle and corrupt," he
could build an effective bridge from the ideal world to the world of real
commonwealths. Thus, while Hythlodaeus urges the reader to contemplate and wish for his Utopian society, More urges the reader to
contemplate and attempt to adjust his life to the attitudes of Utopian
individuals. By this means, man may begin a struggle toward the
perfect state where the effort must begin, in the human personality, not
in the formalized institutions of society.

that virtue has its reward, and yet, with equality of distribution, all men have abundance of all things, and
then when I contrast with their policies the many nations
elsewhere ever making ordinances and yet never one of
them achieving good order . . . I become more partial
to Plato and less surprised at his refusal to make laws
for those who rejected that legislation which gave to all
an equal share in all goods.

"This wise sage, to be sure, easily foresaw that the
one and only road to the general welfare lies in the
maintenance of equality in all respects." (103–05)

Hythlodaeus' use of Plato is totally on the institutional
level. He urges that Plato has shown the way to simplifying
the law, since laws exist only to avoid or settle disputes
and disputes arise out of ownership. He argues that Plato
has discovered the "easy" road to the "general welfare,"
a road which "lies in the *maintenance* of equality in all
respects." By focusing upon the institutional idealism
which may be read in Plato's example, Raphael opens
himself up to several criticisms by More, criticisms which
will lead to a parting of the ways of the philosopher-
prophet and the mediating poet.

One such separation has already been noted: the "easy"
path to truth is really the road to negative truth; it leads to
an idyllic world fit for afternoon conversations like the
one to follow, but it does not lead to any lasting understanding because it is divorced from an existential content.
The "easy" idealism of Plato or Hythlodaeus is refreshing
but temporary, for, in the end, the mind must return to
reality. Beyond this facile quality in Plato read as Raphael
reads him lie some more specific objections. The first objection is that the idealist is misdirected in thinking that the
source of evil lies in a system of ownership rather than in

the corruption of human nature. Hythlodaeus implicitly touches on this criticism when he observes the futility of the law in ownership societies. Aristotle, in his *Politics*, had expressed criticism of those who naively trust in institutional solutions:

> But the real cause of all these evils [lawsuits, etc.] is not the absence of communism, but wickedness, since we see far more quarrels occurring among those who own or use property in common than among those who have their estates separate.[23]

More echoes Aristotle's objection and amplifies it by making pointed reference to the continued necessity of a legal tradition in any society.

> "But," I ventured, "I am of the contrary opinion. Life cannot be satisfactory where all things are common. How can there be a sufficient supply of goods when each withdraws himself from the labor of production? For the individual does not have the motive of personal gain and he is rendered slothful by trusting to the industry of others. Moreover, when people are goaded by want and yet the individual cannot legally keep as his own what he has gained, must there not be trouble from continual bloodshed and riot? This holds true especially since the authority of magistrates and respect for their office have been eliminated, for how there can be any place for these among men who are all on the same level I cannot even conceive." (107)

---

23. *Utopia*, p. 379, quoting Aristotle's *Politics*, 2.2.8–9, 1263b; Surtz also refers the reader to *Politics*, 2.2.13, 1264a and to Aquinas' *Com. in Arist. Pol.* 2.4.

Far from seeing in community of property the easy road to the general welfare, More asserts, like Aristotle before him, that communism tends to corrupt human nature. Community of property destroys the individual character of labor, removes the incentive of personal expression and personal achievement, in effect, negates the ethic of personal liberty which lies at the base of any conception of human dignity. Moreover, by eliminating proprietorship and private ownership, it destroys the foundations of exchange between men and denies man's potential for charitable action and his ability to govern himself. Finally, by equalizing humanity, reducing all men to a common level, community of property destroys the mutual respect founded upon accomplishment and eliminates the opportunity for men to submit willingly to a larger cause. More might agree with Hythlodaeus that these freedoms have been abused, but he cannot accompany Raphael along the "easy" path to an uncorrupted life represented by the radical negation of all man's powers of self-expression merely because many abuse them. That man's conduct must be reformed More will concede to Hythlodaeus; that the reform should begin by uprooting all that is natural to the human personality he does not concede.

Thus, More's objections to Hythlodaeus' radically rational idealism, like Aristotle's objections to praise of Plato's apparent institutional idealism, push the reader beyond the economic foundations of culture to the sources of society which lie in the human personality. The human being begins all social corruption; his wickedness is what turns any organizational principle into an exploiting and debilitating institution. This is the point which Cardinal Morton made in his discussion with Hythlodaeus about legal reform in England. When More raises his objections, at the end of Book I, to Raphael's praise of Utopian communism, he intends the reader to recall this individual rather than institutional responsibility for social corruption. At the same time, the inquisitive and open-ended quality of his objections looks forward to the monologue which is to follow. Hythlodaeus, blinded by his own Utopian vision, cannot understand these requests for a closer examination of this perfect island state. Instead, he responds to doubt by offering his own testimony as proof.

> "I do not wonder," he rejoined, "that it looks this way to you, being a person who has no picture at all, or else a false one, of the situation I mean. But you should have been with me in Utopia and personally seen their manners and customs as I did, for I lived there more than five years and would never have wished to leave except to make known that new world." (107)

The irony of this reply is that though we are going to Utopia and are going "to see personally their manners and customs," we are not going to see them "as [Raphael] did": Hythlodaeus was so overcome by the Utopians that he wished to remain in their imaginary world of seeming perfection; but the man he asks to journey with him back to that ideal—the mediating poet—recognizes that the return to Europe must be made if the journey is to have any meaning at all. What More must seek in Utopian institutions, then, is not a perfected society but the means by which to combat the corrupting influences which attack the human personality in the real world. While Hythlodaeus wishes him to see the grand vista of Utopian institutions, More must look into the minds of the individuals in Utopia and seek out that definition of the self which enables them to cooperate with their institutional traditions without being consumed by them as Hythlodaeus has been.

One final objection may be raised to Hythlodaeus' pre-occupation with the institutional character of the Platonic analogue to Utopia. Raphael concludes that one of the great virtues of this institutional ideal is its ability to *maintain* itself, to preserve itself against all change. The same immutable quality is present in Plato's Ideal State when considered as a literal ideal: "To fulfill its ideal, Plato makes his Republic immune to change: once formed, the pattern of order remains static, as in the insect societies to which it bears a close resemblance."[24] Thus, when the utopian myth is conceived as a final and complete ideal, it becomes a machine designed to coerce and drive out any disturbance of its equilibrium. With its whole meaning placed in its institutions, these institutions must be preserved intact at all costs. Such a formalized ideal, whether it be Plato's or Hythlodaeus', transforms self-discipline into repression, the dictates of the individual conscience into the commands of a social conscience, the welfare of each individual into the welfare of the generality, human nature into the ideal mechanism, struggling and aspiring life into uniform and uninspired death.

Hythlodaeus and More both seek the same end—a return of man in the community to the norms of behavior dictated by his nature and reason. They approach this end, however, from opposite directions. To More the ideal must always preserve the free play of the human will. This freedom engenders the danger of corruption from within and from without, but perfection becomes meaningless when it is divorced from the willing human spirit which is its very subject. To Hythlodaeus, the ideal must first of all maintain itself, for everything depends upon it. His philosophic insight has derived from his psychological commitment to

24. Mumford, p. 275.

the Utopian ideal; therefore, to preserve the hope of perfection he must finally choose to look to the welfare of the ideal before he may look to the manner in which man relates to that ideal. On the other hand, for More the ideal is only a place in the mind, not a place to which he can journey physically; therefore, More and the reader, having journeyed only from the armchair, may look first to their own conscience and to their own consciousness of the ideal. One needs the philosopher-prophet-physician to envision the ideal; but one needs the awareness of the self-disciplined mind to see that man chooses his ideals, the ideals do not choose man. More will travel with his contemplative alter-ego as far as is necessary to glimpse Utopia; from there the constructive potential, the creative act, depends upon man, not the ideal.

# 3

*Utopia,* Book II:

Hythlodaeus' Discourse

and the True Utopia Within

Book I of *Utopia* and More's prefatory letters are de-
voted to defining the proper relationship between the
utopian dreamer and his utopia. The *telos* ideals of a
utopia mesmerize the idealist, enfeebling his powers of
discrimination. Caught up in his utopian vision, the reformer is unable to distinguish ideal from illusion, what is
potentially transferable to the world of political reality
from what belongs to the realm of the imagination. Hythlodaeus is so completely immersed in his philosophic scheme
that his judgment is distorted, his will paralyzed; he longs
to remain in his metaphysical garden of Adonis. The poet
More, through his own participation in the dialogues of
Book I and through the pragmatic insights of Cardinal
Morton, has defined a mediating stance between ideality
and reality which is capable of separating the truth in
Hythlodaeus' ideals from the deceptive illusions which lie
in wait at the seemingly logical extremes of his *telos* myth.
Book II of *Utopia*—the Discourse—presents an even more
difficult problem of mediation. More is still posing the
question of stance toward the utopian myth, but now he
poses it more directly. The reader no longer has a selection
of attitudes toward Utopia from which to choose as he did
in the range of postures defined by Raphael, More, and
Cardinal Morton in the first book; now he confronts the

myth and Hythlodaeus' tale directly, with its mixture of
ideals and illusions left unsorted. The difficulties of interpretation and proper judgment are so imposing that it may
well have been a desire to aid his humanist audience in
distinguishing fact from fiction in Hythlodaeus' scheme
which originally prompted More to add Book I and the
parerga. Indeed, he may have undertaken these later addi-
tions to clarify in his own mind the relationship between
the valuable and the valueless in this dangerously attractive picture of a "perfect" island state. In any case, the
reader now finds himself in a position similar to that of the
hunters and gatherers facing their first experience of the
"divine city": the immediacy of the impression and the
forcefulness of the impact of this *telos* leaves little room for
mediation.

Fortunately, More has provided the reader with an opportunity for judging events in their proper perspective
which the first slaves to a utopian illusion never had. The
reader has in mind the suggestions of the proper posture
toward such mythical ideals that More has developed in the
parerga and Book I and which he has summarized in the
metaphor of a play. Moreover, the framework of the Discourse encourages the reader to detach himself from the
romance of Hythlodaeus' narration and reflect upon its
various dimensions. This detachment is achieved through
the device of a fictional audience, More and Peter Giles,
for what Hythlodaeus relates is told not to the reader but
to them, and More, in turn, conveys it to the reader. The
question which arises is: Why did More use this technique
of recorded narrative? Why does he introduce the mediating poet into the work itself? Why, for example, did he
not reveal the outlines of the Utopian state as Plato did in
the *Republic,* by question and response? Clearly, it would
have been possible to describe all of Utopia by having

Hythlodaeus respond to queries made by Giles and More. To say that Giles and More did not exist as active characters in the *Utopia* as originally conceived is to avoid the issue. Why did not More make his persona and Peter Giles active participants in the revelation of Utopian society? The answers to these questions must lie in the problems posed by the nature of the philosophic ideal Hythlodaeus is preaching and in the character of the philosophic idealist. As has been suggested in the preceding chapters, the utopian idealist merges his whole personality in the utopian *telos*, identifies his own being with the existence of his ideal, and thus transposes both himself and his ideal from the existential world to the essential world, from reality to the realm of the ideal. Thus, to record this development in Hythlodaeus' personality would be only natural; it would be the conclusion of the process which More's letters and Book I have anticipated. Part of the purpose of the distanced, monologic presentation of Utopia, then, is to express this psychological experience, and to allow the mediating poet to record the event while holding himself and the reader aloof from the engulfing result.

This process of the individual losing all perspective in his enthusiasm for the ideal is illustrated in an anecdote which occurs early in the published *Utopia* but which, significantly, preceded the opening of the monologic Discourse in the original version by only sixteen lines.[1]

Their mariners were skilled in adapting themselves to sea and weather. But he [Hythlodaeus] reported that he won their extraordinary favor by showing them the use of the magnetic needle of which they had hitherto been quite ignorant so that they had hesitated to trust them-

1. See Hexter, *Utopia: The Biography*, pp. 18–22 or *Utopia*, pp. xix-xx.

selves to the sea and had boldly done so in the summer only. Now, trusting to the magnet, they do not fear wintry weather, being dangerously confident. Thus, there is a risk that what was thought likely to be a great benefit to them may, through their imprudence, cause them great mischief. (53)

The point of this anecdote is that haste and enthusiasm may turn well-intentioned and benevolent gestures into corrupting gifts.[2] The danger arises that novelty may be taken as evidence of absolute truth and that the morality of the institutional framework may be upset by a too-willing reliance upon the innovation. There is a value in traditional or familiar rituals which cannot be ignored even when the novel idea has greater intrinsic value than the old pattern it replaces. "Whatever play is being performed, perform it as best you can, and do not upset it all simply because you think of another which has more interest," More warns Hythlodaeus (99). May not More be uttering a similar general warning to the reader when he suggests "that what was thought likely to be a great benefit to them may, through their imprudence, cause them great mischief"?

Thus, the anecdote of the "magnetic needle" serves to establish the province of irony which is intended to prevent the reader from agreeing completely with Hythlodaeus; it helps establish the balance the poet is attempting to maintain between the philosopher and the politician. Much like the dialogic structure of Book I, the hidden ironies of Book

2. This does not mean that one should reject a change because of its dangerous consequences, just as the abuse of an institution already in existence and inherently good does not justify completely replacing it (*Utopia*, p. 306). As is frequently the case in *Utopia*, More's attitude is refined: he continually distinguishes between the manner in which some institution is used and the absolute value of that institution.

II detach the poet and the reader from Hythlodaeus' totally unconscious involvement in his vision. These ironies are the means by which More hopes to enable the reader to distinguish Raphael's instructive ideals from the destructive illusions of his *telos* myth. These ironic dissonances, however, do not mean that all of Utopia or all of Hythlodaeus' idealism must be discounted. In fact, Raphael's ability to envision the ideal as well as the content of what he envisions is meant to engage the reader and to earn his qualified approval. The qualification depends upon the mediating poet who determines, from his detachment, not only what may be seen of Utopia and Hythlodaeus but also what may be seen of how they interrelate and define each other. Therefore, not all of what Hythlodaeus sees nor all of what he praises is the province of irony; the irony extends only to the manner in which Utopia and Hythlodaeus act upon each other to the exclusion of any personal fulfillment through mutually and willingly exercised freedom and duty. For Hythlodaeus as the idealist, the province of irony is the consuming of his individuality by the institutions of Utopia; for Utopia as a system, the realm of ironic condemnation is the illusion of perfection which is accomplished only by crushing the Utopian individual in the state's drive to preserve itself as a coherent, uniform ideal. The preliminary journey through Utopia, then, must do two things through the monologue: it must introduce the reader to what potentially ennobles the individual in Utopia and what is engaging in Hythlodaeus' idealism; it must also reveal the province of irony— what potentially degrades the individual in Utopian society and what is disenchanting about Raphael's engulfing vision. While noting the constructive potential contained in the Utopian system revealed in this initial peregrination around the island, it will be necessary, in order to explain the complex irony of the monologue, to focus upon the potential degeneration which exists in the ultimately false way that Hythlodaeus becomes a mere adjunct of his rationalism and the ultimately negative manner in which he arrives at the illusion of a common agreement—by depersonalizing human nature.

Hythlodaeus introduces the reader (and More) to Utopia topographically. Even in these neutral details, presented in a relatively flat tone, one may detect qualities which, while they suggest a vision of perfect man in perfected society, nevertheless betray Hythlodaeus' susceptibility to ignoring the self when confronted with a convenient rationalism. In the first place, Utopia is isolated and impregnable:

> The mouth of this bay is rendered perilous here by shallows and there by reefs. Almost in the center of the gap stands one great crag which, being visible, is not dangerous. A tower built on it is occupied by a garrison. The other rocks are hidden and therefore treacherous. The channels are known only to the natives, and so it does not easily happen that any foreigner enters the bay except with a Utopian pilot. (111)

What makes this naturally defensible position of Utopia ominously treacherous is not the simple fact of geographical inapproachability, but the conspiracy between man and nature to enhance this isolation:

> In fact, the entrance is hardly safe even for themselves, unless they guide themselves by landmarks on the shore. If these were removed to other positions, they could easily lure an enemy's fleet, however numerous, to destruction. (111)

Moreover, though there are many seaside harbors, their landings are "so well defended by nature or by engineering that a few defenders can prevent strong forces from coming ashore" (111). Finally, Utopus, the man responsible for "such a perfection of culture and humanity as makes them now superior to almost all other mortals," contrived after his victory to sever Utopia permanently from its continental connections by a fifteen-mile channel (113). In other words, to a large extent Utopia's perfection is founded upon a discontinuity with its past—an isolation which parallels the drastic alienation from the arena of political compromise reflected in Hythlodaeus' philosophic convictions.

Hythlodaeus next proceeds to a description of the organization of the Utopian community. Utopia is an island of "fifty-four city-states, all spacious and magnificent, identical in language, traditions, customs, and laws" (113). Uniformity, not intercourse between differentiated entities, lies at the center of this Utopian ideal of perfection. Ritual is not the result of individual evolutions; rather, it follows from a planned and decreed similarity. There is nothing organic about Utopia's history: mutability has been eliminated; change has been arrested; life is truly man-made, an engineering project on a grand scale which will move a whole forest for convenience (179). When man is allowed to plan his own life, he is able to cope with the problems of existence in his own way. When society takes from him the necessity of ordering his life, it may make existence more convenient, but it also renders life unreal. Again, then, there is the potential in rational planning to make man a mere social fixture rather than to make society the scaffolding on which man is able to express his communal instincts.

At the heart of this larger political unit one finds the

Utopian family.[3] The household represents at one and the same time a great extension and a great limitation of the familial principle. On the one hand, the potential bonds of family affection are extended to a greater number of people: "No rural household numbers less than forty men and women" (115). On the other hand, the continuity of family communications is completely broken down:

> Twenty from each household return every year to the city, namely, those having completed two years in the country. As substitutes in their place, the same number are sent from the city. (115)

Each year the family is halved, part remaining in the country, part returning to the city. There is consolation in the fact that occupations await each person at both ends of the social assembly line and that social products will continue to flow from the factory. But one might legitimately wonder if the sense of utility and security fostered by this convenient mobility rivals the sense of contribution and appreciation embodied in the more traditional family unit. A

---

3. The role of the family in *Utopia* is central. Indeed, while More borrowed many ideas from Plato (though often only after turning them around to focus upon the *means* an ideal may disclose rather than the *end* which it enshrines), he completely rejected Plato's community of wives in favor of a more traditional familial organization. "More incorporated so many traits of Plato's *polis* in *Utopia* that his rejection of the most striking of these traits [community of wives] could hardly have been the result of anything but conscious choice" *(Utopia,* p. xliv). One possible reason for retaining the household familiar to his contemporaries (see George Cavendish, *Life & Death of Cardinal Wolsey,* ed. Richard Sylvester, EETS, os 243 [Oxford, 1959], p. 104, for the equivalence between the extended "family" and the "household" in sixteenth-century England) as the central institution of Utopian society may have been to shift interest from a novel form to concern with the means of realizing the benefits inherent in the common institutions of life.

particularly clever insight into the supposition underlying this blueprint is contained in the anecdote which immediately follows the above passage:

> The hens do not brood over the eggs, but the farmers, by keeping a great number of them at a uniform heat, bring them to life and hatch them. As soon as they come out of the shell, the chicks follow and acknowledge humans as their mothers! (115)

In a similar way the Utopian incubator processes people, for when all is equal what difference can possibly exist between one parent and another? Thus, in the Utopian family, which Hythlodaeus presents as the center of their communistic society, there exists the potential for development in either of two directions. The expression of all aspects of life through the family may introduce the patterns of affectionate behavior characteristic of the nuclear family into all forms of social conduct. The standardizing and mechanizing of the family, the interchanging of its parts, on the other hand, may lead to degrading and devaluing the human personality. The choice is still open, but the danger signals have already begun to appear. The problem left to the mediating poet and the reader is to determine where and how the constructive ideal transforms itself into an illusion capable of destroying the basic values of humanity.

From a cursory introductory portrait Hythlodaeus proceeds to a more specific examination of the island, concentrating particularly upon the capital city, Amaurotum. The most important institution in the city-state is its government, and the family unit, again, is the basis of oganization. Highest in the political hierarchy is a governor, elected for life "unless ousted on suspicion of aiming at a tyranny"; next come the protophylarchs or tranibors who "are elected annually but are not changed without good reason"; finally, there are the phylarchs or syphogrants who hold office only for one year (123). The government is carefully arranged to avoid tyranny and conspiracies against itself.

The object of these measures, they say, is to prevent it from being easy, by a conspiracy between the governor and the tranibors and by tyrannous oppression of the people, to change the order of the commonwealth. Therefore whatever is considered important is laid before the assembly of the syphogrants who, after informing their groups of families, take counsel together and report their decision to the senate. Sometimes the matter is laid before the council of the whole island. (125)

Though More might very much approve such direct representation, he would also be aware of its political limitations, especially for a nation-state like England. Beyond this, however, the purpose of these elaborate checks on the legislative power of the syphogrants is unclear, for, if uniformity among the city-states is to be maintained, the legislative capacity of these institutions must be quite limited; probably it merely extends their judicial role—deciding the few disputes between private persons (123). In any case, few laws are passed "because very few are needed" (195). This paucity of necessary laws arises from Raphael's philosophic postulate of an all-pervasive rationality. Yet although one might appreciate this philosophic blessing of uncorrupted reason "in the private conversation of close friends" (99), in the real world where, as Morton reminds the reader, one is as apt to find evil men as good, such freedom from law and tradition may well lead to a tyranny founded upon the caprice of the magistrates—a tyranny more insidious than oppression because its application is unpredictable.

The Utopian provisions against tyrannical usurpation echo a longing frequently articulated by More:

> Nothing is clearer, when we look through More's Latin poems, most of them written in the years when the *Richard* [and the *Utopia*] was being planned and composed, than the profound interest which the problem of tyranny had aroused in the mind of the young poet.[4]

But if More could appreciate the wisdom of attempting to extirpate tyranny, he could also be chilled by the costs implied in the ease with which the philosophic state solves the problem of the tyrant. The Utopians, in creating rules which prevent factions from usurping power, lose, in that process, the positive values of factionalism—the values of pluralism. Thus, the measures which suppress factionalism in Utopia also legislate out all change and substitute a proclaimed uniformity for the organic features of a pluralistic society. What Hythlodaeus constantly overlooks as he views Utopia is that the ease with which some measure eliminates an inconvenient corruption may be purchased at the great cost of some important dimension of the human personality.

The discussion of Utopian occupations again presents a world of mixed blessings. Agriculture is an occupation common to all. "Besides agriculture . . . each is taught one particular craft as his own. This is generally either woolworking or linen-making or masonry or metal-working or carpentry" (125). The correspondence between this pro-

4. Sylvester, *Richard III*, p. xcix.

gram and Hythlodaeus' response to the lawyer at Cardinal
Morton's table is striking. In both instances crafts are emphasized as a means to express the liberty and value implicit in human nature. On this level, then, the universal
compulsion to work is a force enhancing human potential and liberating individual expression. Moreover, the
method of learning a craft coincides with the principles of
family affection as opposed to factory depersonalization.[5]

> For the most part, each is brought up in his father's
> craft, for which most have a natural inclination. But if
> anyone is attracted to another occupation, he is trans-
> ferred by adoption to a family pursuing that craft for
> which he has a liking. Care is taken not only by his
> father but by the authorities, too, that he will be as-
> signed to a grave and honorable householder. More-
> over, if anyone after being thoroughly taught one craft
> desires another also, the same permission is given. (127)

Thus, the Utopians seem to recognize the values of the
familial economy, the virtues of affectionate instruction,
the benefits of learning trades that, in some sense, are
menial, "but not as a menial."[6] The singular blessing of
such a system, however, again is clouded by the creeping
shadow of utilitarianism and mechanization. Having acquired both trades, the Utopian citizen "practices his
choice unless the city has more need of the one than of the
other" (127). One cannot quite escape the fact that labor
does not attain a free and independent value in Utopia.
The individual ethic of work is constantly impinged upon
by the needs and plans of the society.

5. For a discussion of this aspect of preindustrial society in Europe
see Peter Laslett, *The World We Have Lost* (New York, 1965).
   6. Chambers, *Thomas More,* p. 60.

That work is social due rather than self-expression is shown even more clearly in the policy that "idle persons [will] be driven from the commonwealth" (127).

> The chief and almost the only function of the sypho-grants is to manage and provide that no one sit idle, but that each apply himself industriously to his trade, and yet that he be not wearied like a beast of burden with constant toil from early morning till late at night. (127)

By enforcing a universal participation the Utopians elimi-nate social deadweight and free workers from enchain-ment to the soil. In the process, however, they subvert other qualities in their society. Hythlodaeus perceives the efforts of the Utopians to free man from a slavery to the soil, but he does not see that, in ignoring the individual and independent character of labor consonant with human nature and in subordinating labor to a socially utilitarian end, they may condemn man to an institutional slavery. Similarly, the syphogrants, who were introduced as legis-lators, turn out to be, almost completely, extensions of the administrative or coercive arm of the government. They constitute part of a graded bureaucracy whose job it is to see that the social machine runs well. They too are slaves of the institution they serve.

The Utopians spend much of their leisure time in intel-lectual activities, often attending predawn lectures (129). Their recreations are innocent. They spend summers in their gardens, winters in their common halls, and have music to accompany their after-dinner conversations. There is neither dicing nor any other game of chance; rather, their games are meant to be profitable as well as pleasant (129). Extending this satiric contrast to Euro-pean frivolousness further, Hythlodaeus attacks the idleness and luxury which force the poor in Europe to work so hard to support the noble classes (131). In contrast to the thousands of idle in Europe, very few are exempted from labor in Utopia and these only to pursue education or religion (131–33). Indeed, all social practices cooperate in this efficiency drive: houses are generally repaired rather than rebuilt and clothes are of a simple and uniform quality and limited to only the essential garments (133–35).

This picture of the everyday activities of its citizens reveals an important aspect of Utopia: to a large extent the institutions (the family, the various village assemblies, the apprenticeship program in the trades), the gardens, the simple amusements, would be familiar to the Englishman of More's day. If this is the case, the important question More raises is not what new institutional panacea (like community of property) does Europe need in order to move toward Utopia but rather what change in the attitudes of men would make life better. One should recall two facts which bear upon this problem. The first is the origin of *Utopia,* which More emphasized in his letters— life's everyday demands, man's consciousness of his obligations to family and friends, his understanding of right action done in good conscience. The second is Mumford's argument that the historic origin of utopianism lies in the transmogrification of the common institutions of the hunting-and-gathering village culture into the mythic-religious forms of the holy, princely city. More's solution leads to a flexible pattern of life which naturally expresses man's role in a social context. The historical genesis of utopianism leads logically to the dehumanization of man and the creation of a totalitarian, collective machine. It is this directional ambiguity which underlines the paradox of the Utopian *telos* myth. Though the form of the utopia to which the poet More would wish to lead his humanistic audience may closely parallel the structure of the Utopia Hythlodaeus has seen, there is a crucial difference in emphasis—the difference between looking for the solution in reformed individuals and seeking it in radically rational institutions. In the former all sanctions rest with the individual conscience; in the latter the only sanction is for the preservation of the philosophic ideal intact. This is the same distinction More maintained in Book I when he advised "performing the play at hand" over accepting a novel play which seems to have greater intrinsic value (99). In other words, the only foundation upon which man may distinguish the value of an ideal from the deception of an illusory wish is the history of human experiences. These guidelines of shared human experiences Thomas More must reveal in Hythlodaeus' narrative if any ideals are to emerge from Raphael's utopian illusion.

The next section of Hythlodaeus' tale is his description of Utopian "Social Relations." "Households as a rule are made up of those related by blood" (135). Family organization is patrilineal, brides moving into the homes of their husbands (135). However distinct the lines of descent may be in the beginning, they quickly become blurred by transferring persons from one household to another to maintain the population balance (137).[7] Thus the role of father, for instance, is more functional than natural. A child would consider that person to be his father who occupies the position of father in his household, whether the father is his actual progenitor or not. Properly implemented, this policy would not necessarily destroy the affections between members of the family, but then that

7. As Surtz notes *(Utopia,* p. 415), one cannot be certain whether children are included in this population transference. But even if it is limited to adults, the effect on the family remains the same—to break up familial connections.

proper implementation resembles very closely the equation of the conduct of chickens in an incubator with that of human beings in a social chicken coop. Thus, though on the simply descriptive level the bonds of familial affection seem to be retained and extended to greater numbers, the inference on a deeper level seems to be that Hythlodaeus might be very willing to see natural family bonds replaced by artificial ties, if that were found necessary in order to preserve the Utopian ideal intact and render it safe from human error.

Though the Utopians, through community of property, have no personal sense of ownership, they develop a very strong sense of communal possession. The right to social ownership they feel justified in expressing whenever population pressures make it expedient:

> And if the population throughout the island should happen to swell above the fixed quotas, they enroll citizens out of every city and, on the mainland nearest them, wherever the natives have much unoccupied and uncultivated land, they found a colony under their own laws. . . . By their procedures they make the land sufficient for both, which previously seemed poor and barren to the natives. The inhabitants who refuse to live according to their laws, they drive from the territory which they carve out for themselves. If they resist, they wage war against them. They consider it a most just cause for war when a people which does not use its soil but keeps it idle and waste nevertheless forbids the use and possession of it to others who by the rule of nature ought to be maintained by it. (137)

Though the action of the Utopians may make land that was lying in waste fertile and productive, it asserts a "rule of nature" equivalent to "might makes right." This example, more clearly than any of the preceding incidents of social utilitarianism in the Discourse, reveals how the Utopian ideal of community overrides traditional human values in its drive toward a smooth and convenient life.

The issue, however, is again made unclear when the descriptive focus shifts to domestic social relations. The Utopians pool all social goods in public storehouses and may freely take what is needed (137).

> Why should anything be refused? First, there is a plentiful supply of all things and, secondly, there is no underlying fear that anyone will demand more than he needs. Why should there be any suspicion that someone may demand an excessive amount when he is certain of never being in want? No doubt about it, avarice and greed are aroused in every kind of living creature by the fear of want, but only in man are they motivated by pride alone—pride which counts it a personal glory to excel others by superfluous display of possessions. The latter vice can have no place at all in the Utopian scheme of things. (139)

On the one hand, insecurity, a feeling shared by all creatures, may create the demand for superfluous goods. Such anxiety the Utopian scheme of things eliminates by assuring that all that is *needed* will be supplied. This it does both by insuring universal participation in producing goods and by limiting wants. On the other hand, man alone seeks a superabundance of objects out of pride. Utopian society eliminates pride through the same techniques of discipline. The key to this happy existence, as More would see it, is not merely discipline but a properly conceived and applied self-discipline. Is Hythlodaeus willing to allow man this self-governing freedom, or, if given the choice between the individual and the society, would he be willing to coerce society's members into approved conduct in order to preserve his communistic ideal?

The hierarchy of position at dinner reveals the means used by the Utopians to inculcate respect for elders and uniformity of behavior. All children below the age of marriage either serve their superiors or stand by silently waiting for their portions to be handed them from their elders' tables (143). At each table the younger persons are scattered in among those older and more grave.

The reason for this practice, they say, is that the grave and reverend behavior of the old may restrain the younger people from mischievous freedom in word and gesture, since nothing can be done or said at table which escapes the notice of the old present on every side. (143)

Thus an example of proper conduct is kept before the young at even the most casual moments. Furthermore, the older men are served first and with the best food. At their discretion they may "give a share of their delicacies to their neighbors" (145). In this way the proper respect is given to seniority, yet equality is preserved among all. Before meals an appropriate moral lesson is read. During the meals the elders initiate conversations on approved subjects and try to draw out the young and to test their characters (145). To "cheer the company," music is played, spices burnt and perfumes scattered. "For they are somewhat too much inclined to this attitude of mind: that no kind of pleasure is forbidden, provided no harm comes of it" (145).[8] In other words, with very few pleasures, and these only natural ones, the Utopians must derive their enjoyment from vir-

8. As Clarence Miller has observed, "Though there may be a 'note of disapproval' (as Father Surtz says in his note, *Utopia,* p. 424) in the phrase 'sunt enim hanc in partem aliquanto procliuiores' (144/20–21), there is no justification for 'too much' in the translation: 'For they are

tuous conduct itself. Whether this manner of pleasure is the willing choice of each Utopian or the result of having no alternative, whether their rigorous diet of authority and discipline makes virtue a growth from within or a quality imposed and protected by the state, whether the common interest emerges from the sum of individual interests or coerces the individual into agreement with it, are questions which the re-creation of Hythlodaeus' psychological growth toward the Utopian ideal has raised without answering definitively. To answer these questions, to distinguish between More's and Hythlodaeus' intended emphases, requires a second journey through this ideal island —a journey which commences with the issuing of the customary and mandatory Utopian travel pass (145).

The introductory journey through Utopia, with Hythlodaeus as guide, has accomplished two purposes. It has indicated the singularly important role of the family in Utopian culture, and it has re-created, symbolically, Raphael's psychological growth into the Utopian society. The reader has seen the institutions and the hope for man that Raphael envisioned in the Utopian state. He has also seen how Hythlodaeus has lost his ability to discriminate between the ends to which Utopia is directed and the means that are to be used by the Utopians to achieve those ends. In each Utopian institution, founded as it is upon

---

somewhat too much inclined to this attitude of mind.' 'Aequo' or 'iusto' is not to be understood with 'procliuiores,' which simply means 'more inclined' to this position ('that no kind of pleasure is forbidden, provided no harm comes of it') than to the opposite, ascetic view of pleasure" (Miller, "The English Translation in the Yale *Utopia:* Some Corrections," *Moreana, 9* [February 1966], 58). Though Hythlodaeus here introduces only a vague misgiving about the Utopians' preference for pleasure, he still ends his appraisal of their ethic by misunderstanding and disapproving it.

discipline, there exists a directional ambiguity: discipline may be self-applied by each Utopian citizen and grow out of his willingness to aspire toward a common agreement, or discipline may spread down from repressive institutions designed to hold society to the perfect goal which is the philosopher's ideal. Hythlodaeus has gradually lost his ability to discriminate between these alternatives because he has lost his desire to concern himself with the means to perfection; he has become totally preoccupied with the ends to which man should aspire. He has lost his individualism in his idealism, and he thus opens the way to the risk that the individual will be forfeited to the preservation of the institutional ideal originally created by the individual. More signals Raphael's subsuming of his personality in his social idealism by recording the faint note of doubt in Hythlodaeus' appraisal of Utopia: "For they are somewhat too much inclined to this attitude of mind: that no kind of pleasure is forbidden, provided no harm comes of it" (145). What is crucial in the growth of Raphael's disapproval is that this conception of pleasure is the very means by which each Utopian individual is able to agree with the common Utopian cause. In the discussion which follows this introduction of Hythlodaeus' misgiving—"Utopian Travel"— the reader does not journey around Utopia as the title might suggest; rather, he is asked to consider how one moves from the familiar rituals of his life to the Utopian pattern Raphael is suggesting. Hythlodaeus, trapped by the rationalism which his description applies to all Utopian activities, sees the solution as lying only in a rationally integrated institutional framework. Because the reader confronts Raphael's narrative, not as he first tells it but as it is relayed through the fictional Thomas More, a certain distance is achieved. Reminded by More's mediating presence of all that he has said in his letters to Peter Giles and in Book I, the reader must balance in his own mind what he sees of the Utopians with his own experiences of life. This examination of the ethical system of the Utopians ironically undercuts the very aspects of the island which have elicited Hythlodaeus' enthusiasm and shifts the exploration away from goals to means—the attitudes of mind —which the Utopians employ in attaining and adjusting to their ideal. An understanding of the evolution of the Utopian ethic of pleasure and of the ties which bind it to each individual's conscience becomes the means by which More and the reader are able to borrow from Hythlodaeus' vision only those elements which truly work toward a better society and to reject those elements in Raphael's tale which lead to the mesmerizing illusion of perfection.

Hythlodaeus suggests within what limits the ironic distance between himself and More is to develop when he observes that "the whole island is like a single family" (149). The principle of the family lies at the origin of Utopian perfection, but Raphael's growing confusion over the meaning of the family in the Utopian institutional hierarchy turns this statement around into a question: what kind of family is this whole island like? As the discussion of the Utopian system of ethics proceeds, and as Raphael detaches himself from the *means* presented in that system for preserving the values of the individual within the institutions of the family and the state, it becomes increasingly clear that Hythlodaeus' loss of himself to his ideal has impaired his vision. In Hythlodaeus' view, the family becomes founded on negations and most importantly on the negation of property in communism. Increasingly, he turns away from the familial principle and toward these negative ideals because their coercion helps the state survive. On the other hand, More constructs his perspective as the mediating poet on the foundation provided by

this Utopian ethical system and thereby creates the basis
upon which he will correct Hythlodaeus' definition of the
Utopian *telos.* To More, the family reflects the creative
potential of the human personality; most importantly, it
expresses the notion of reasonable man joining willingly
with his fellows in a community—the goal which the
Epicurean-Stoic ethic of the Utopians is designed to
achieve. Thus, a second journey into Utopia is initiated,
and the reader is meant to be guided by the questions which
the irony underlying Hythlodaeus' description raises. Because the author has imposed himself as a fictional audience between Raphael and the reader, we are led past
Hythlodaeus' Utopia to an ideal which includes the realm
of practical experience that More, the mediating poet,
brings to the monologue.

The introduction into this second exploratory probe of
Utopia is accomplished by examining customs involving
the traditional measures of material prosperity, gold and
silver. While Hythlodaeus focuses on the Utopians' seemingly paranoid rejection of gold and silver, he touches
only in passing upon a more important insight, one which
More will soon develop.

> To gold and silver, however, nature has given no use
> that we cannot dispense with, if the folly of men had not
> made them valuable because they are rare. On the other
> hand, like a most kind and indulgent mother, she has
> exposed to view all that is best, like air and water and
> earth itself, but has removed as far as possible from
> us all vain and unprofitable things. (151)

This analysis presents two principles: the first substitutes
utility for rareness as a source of value. The ambiguity of
such a principle of value is that one cannot be sure to what
end utility will be applied. The second principle assumes

that nature is benign, that what is possessed in common is the best source of community. In this principle one may find both the measure of value—commonness—and its source—nature. The difference between these two theories of value constitutes the essential difference between Hythlodaeus' vision and More's. Raphael, involved in Utopian community of property, constantly returns to the usefulness of that ideal for solving problems which seem to entrap other people. More, from his detached perspective, seeks a more refined, though perhaps less efficient, commonness than community of property—that which is by nature common to all. Hythlodaeus pursues community of property in its specific, More in its generic, meaning.

The growing disaffection between Hythlodaeus and More climaxes in the presentation of Utopian ethics. Hythlodaeus feels that the Utopians base their notion of happiness too much upon pleasure. "In this matter they seem to lean more than they should to the school that espouses pleasure as the object by which to define either the whole or the chief part of human happiness" (161). In fact, the Utopian creed—their synthesis of virtue and pleasure—rests on a distinction between "natural" and "unnatural" pleasures. In turn, this distinction between natural and unnatural derives from their basic religious principles. Again, Hythlodaeus finds this line of reasoning incomprehensible: "What is more astonishing is that they seek a defense for this soft doctrine from their religion, which is serious and strict, almost solemn and hard" (161).[9] Hythlodaeus not only dissociates himself from the issues of this ethical discussion by hedging his praise and by professing

9. "As in other passages (e.g., 144/20–21, 160/21, 178/12–15), Hythlodaeus here dissociates himself subtly from the conceptual base of the ethical theory dominant in Utopia. The contrast between reservations in the area of ethical theory and the absence of such reservations

his inability to understand the argument; at the end of the discussion—which runs for eighteen pages—he refuses, *for the only time in the Discourse,* to defend the Utopians.

This is their view of virtue and pleasure. They believe that human reason can attain to no truer view, unless a heaven-sent religion inspire man with something more holy. Whether in this stand they are right or wrong, time does not permit us to examine—nor is it necessary. We have taken upon ourselves only to describe their principles, and not also to defend them. (179)[10]

---

in the area of social and economic institutions is noteworthy and significant" *(Utopia,* p. 444). What is perhaps most noteworthy and significant about Hythlodaeus' dissociation from the *means* of reform embodied in the Utopian ethic and his identification with the *ends* embodied in Utopian institutions is that his concern with portraying a final goal has blinded him to any conceptual base which might be transferable to the real world he has so abruptly left behind.

10. The use of the "we" construction is very interesting. The first person plural is used in several instances in the Discourse. In some cases it refers to Europeans (see 153, 159, 161); in some cases it applies to human nature in general (see 163, 165, 173, 175); in some cases it designates Raphael and his companions during their stay in Utopia (see 181, 183). But the above use of "we" seems to be the only instance when it is employed in the Discourse as an editorial form. The significance of this fact is that it condenses two crucial questions—the problem of stance and the problem of truth in *Utopia.* The problem of stance leads ultimately to the query: what in *Utopia* is congruent with the author's attitudes? More underlines this problem in the second letter to Giles when he says: "I would only have them [the readers of *Utopia*] understand that I am responsible for my own work alone and not also for the credit of another" (253). A more important reference to the author's attitude toward his *Utopia* occurs when Raphael invites More to return with him to that island and observe the Utopians' "manners and customs as [he] did" (107). The irony of that invitation seems to be echoed in the use of "we" here, for the mediating poet More is seeking, in Utopia, the means by which to translate the ideals of Utopian conduct back into real society; he is not seeking to defend all of Utopian institutional idealism as is Hythlodaeus. Thus, while Hythlodaeus is using the "we" to dissociate himself from the ethical theory of the

This is patently untrue. Raphael undertook the narrative to defend, and not simply to defend but to praise, Utopian institutions.

> I am fully persuaded that no just and even distribution of goods can be made and that no happiness can be found in human affairs unless private property is utterly abolished. While it lasts, there will always remain a heavy and inescapable burden of poverty and misfortunes for by far the greatest and by far the best part of mankind. (105)

---

Utopians in favor of their rationalized institutionalism, the author may be using the "we" to suggest that it is here, with the Utopian means for ordering their lives, that he wishes to begin his true defense of *Utopia*.

As Surtz notes, this passage (and the use of the first person plural) also is crucial for understanding the truths expressed through the Utopian vision: "Hythlodaeus seems to elucidate his attitude thus: 'No matter how most Utopians may *reason* about pleasure, no matter what they may *say* about philosophical foundations, there can be no doubt about the goodness and happiness of their way of life. Their practice is the very best: maybe their theory does not really count' " *(Utopia,* p. 464). This is fine as long as one understands that their practice should be viewed as embodying a *spirit* of action, not enshrining a *pattern* of conduct. But, of course, the danger of Hythlodaeus' idealism, the danger of his ignoring the means to an ideal end (as embodied in the Utopian theory of ethics), is that the pattern, the fruits, may come to monopolize the mind's attention to the exclusion of the spirit, the tree, from which the fruits spring. Again, one is invited to contrast this statement of Hythlodaeus' preoccupation with Utopia as a model with the invitation he issues to More to journey with him to that island state. "Hythlodaeus' answer is practical, not theoretical. He points to the *res,* the reality: Utopia, a supremely successful communistic state" *(Utopia,* p. 382). The irony is that Utopia is not reality but fiction. By pointing to the *res,* Hythlodaeus is only pointing to the Nowhere of the mind. One can only conclude that the editorial "we" serves to underline the distinction between Hythlodaeus' misplaced emphasis on Utopia as a model and More's focus upon the spirit which Utopians employ in their *reasoning* on pleasure—the only "fact" which can eventually be transplanted from the mind to the real world of Europe.

Nor does Raphael have any second thoughts about his desire to defend the Utopians. His concluding words stand as a challenge to all other principles, to all other schemes of things.

> Pride is too deeply fixed in men to be easily plucked out. For this reason, the fact that this form of a commonwealth—which I should gladly desire for all—has been the good fortune of the Utopians at least, fills me with joy. They have adopted such institutions of life as have laid the foundations of the commonwealth not only most happily, but also to last forever, as far as human prescience can forecast. (245)

Moreover, Hythlodaeus has, especially in the "Dialogue of Counsel" of Book I, alienated himself from the world for the sake of his principles, the principles he chooses to illustrate through the institutions of the Utopians. Finally, he presents the Utopian commonwealth as the concrete realization of his principles, and his attachment to Utopia reflects the strength of his convictions. Indeed, this is the very core of the dramatic attraction of his character. Unfortunately, the dramatic attractiveness of Raphael's smooth and easy idealism is also the source of the great dangers which accompany the utopian myth as a defined model for conduct. The radical character of an ideal program (reflected in Raphael's demand that current institutions be "utterly abolished") signals the first danger of Utopia, for defining a goal that may legitimately claim everyone's allegiance is the task of generations reflecting upon their history, their traditions, their limitations as human beings, not a project to be trusted to men guided only by a vision. The natural products of this radicalism—intolerance of critical review of the ideal program ("time does not permit us to examine" the Utopians' reasonings) and transference of faith from people to programs ("They have adopted such *institutions* of life as have laid the foundations of the commonwealth not only most happily, but also to last forever"—italics mine) confirm that Hythlodaeus' attractiveness lies in the force with which he supports his convictions, not in the truth of these attitudes themselves. The directional ambiguity in Raphael's stance toward Utopia is here dissipated; by affirming the Utopian institutional pattern he refuses to take up the real challenge of his idealism: how may the individual human being act to "profit people both as private individuals and as members of the commonwealth" (55).

Thus, in dissociating himself from the ethical beliefs of the Utopians, Hythlodaeus falls prey to the illusion of the Utopians' perfection. His psychological involvement in the Utopian ideal has blinded him to the existential problem of means—how does one go from the individual to the common cause without destroying the meaning of being a man. Therefore, when the discussion shifts from defining ideals for man to analyzing how man might attempt to reach a common agreement with his fellows, the initiative moves away from the self-deceiving idealist to the poet mediating between man and his ideals; the initiative moves from Raphael Hythlodaeus to Thomas More.

The first important fact to understand about the Utopian philosophy of pleasure is that it develops from religious principles. "Without these principles they think reason insufficient and weak by itself for the investigation of true happiness" (161). Though reason will be their guide in developing their philosophy of pleasure, some means is needed to help the Utopians understand their reason, to help them see the rationale behind the efficacy of human reason.

The following are examples of these principles. The soul is immortal and by the goodness of God born for happiness. After this life rewards are appointed for our virtues and good deeds, punishment for our crimes. (161–63)

These two principles of religion are the most important bases of their ethics. They circumscribe the realm wherein man may control his fate. Beyond these two principles, however, lies a third which, together with the other two, defines their "minimal religion." This third belief affirms the role of divine providence in human affairs. Upon these three beliefs rests the "dignity of human nature" (221). The key role of religion in their philosophy explains how pleasure may be the summum bonum of life. Grounding their ethical system in religion they make reason the "servant to faith, not enemy."[11] Thus, the Utopian ethic combines philosophic reason and reasonable religion, and the result of this union is the creed which joins pleasure to virtue.

With a foundation firmly established in religion, reason becomes that particular endowment of man which enables

11. O'Sullivan, "Social Theories," p. 51. For a suggestive discussion of how the Utopian ethical system is integrated into More's social philosophy, the entire article should be consulted. A key element in this integration is the role of reason as handmaiden to faith. More affirms his belief "in the mutual assistance between the reason of philosophy and the faith of theology" in several of his works (see *Utopia*, pp. 444–45, 527). The importance of this cooperation between man's reason and the truths of supernatural religion is that reason (and thus the "natural" ethic of the Utopians) can become a means by which man not only may strive toward the goals which God has designed for human life but also may perceive that these divine truths are congruent with the best side of his nature.

him to express his natural inclinations and grounds these natural inclinations in a tendency to lead the gracious life that "is the perfection of nature."[12]

> The Utopians define virtue as living according to nature since to this end we were created by God. That individual, they say, is following the guidance of nature who, in desiring one thing and avoiding another, obeys the dictates of reason. (163)

In other words, the entire synthesis depends upon two interlocking definitions—the definitions of "reason" and "nature." Philosophic reason is the same as that reason which leads to faith. Philosophic nature is that natural inclination in man which leads to the gracious life. Thus, "reason" and "nature" become bridges; just as they span the gap between religion and philosophy, so too do they join pleasure and virtue. The important fact to grasp is that this is not simply a semantic trick. Thomas More, through the Utopians, is representing these qualities as the right reason and the true nature of man. The remainder of the ethical discussion is a careful explanation of how these qualities may be kept in their uncorrupted state. Very simply, then, the Utopian philosophy of pleasure does not establish the union between virtue and pleasure through the agents of reason and nature; like a true ethical system it assumes this union valid and seeks to preserve its potential uncorrupted by reality while becoming part of it. Utopian philosophy does not attempt to define an end that will replace the goal given in Christian revelation; rather, it attempts to outline a means, proved relevant through its foundation in human reason, by which man may order his conduct toward this end.

12. Ibid., p. 51.

The first rule of conduct derived from the axiomatic relationship between reason and nature is that "reason first of all inflames men to a love and veneration of the divine majesty, to whom we owe both our existence and our capacity for happiness" (163). Man's philosophic reason first leads him to revere that religious force which gave birth to man's total potential. Such a belief is merely a reflection of human nature back upon its source, sanctifying the integrity of its connection with the divine. The affinity between man and God has been impaired perhaps, but the potential lies in man, with God's grace, to return to an uncorrupted union between himself and the divinity. All other derivations from the union of pleasure and virtue look forward to defending this agreement against corruptions growing out of the human personality itself. The first possible perversion of this union occurs when man disregards his communal ties. Therefore, the Utopian ethic affirms man's personal obligation to the community, an obligation which derives from self-fulfillment:

> it admonishes and urges us to lead a life as free from care and as full of joy as possible and, because of our natural fellowship, to help all other men, too, to attain that end. (163)

The crux of this communal impulse is its personal character. Each citizen derives his respect for his fellow egoistically, that is, from a consideration of his own welfare. Nature bids each man seek his own pleasure. In doing so, his personal fulfillment will lead him to a concern for the welfare and pleasure of others; and vice versa, a concern for others naturally leads him back to a healthy concern for himself. The spirit of such an ideal is clearly very close to the attitude expressed in Christian charity.

The danger in such an opinion is that an individual might regard the interests of others as conflicting with his own. Reason and nature, however, counsel him not to measure his own advantage according to the disadvantage of others (165). Right reason will prove that to take from others is really to take from oneself and, conversely, to give to others is to give to oneself.

> On the contrary, to take away something from yourself and to give it to others is a duty of humanity and kindness which never takes away as much advantage as it brings back. It is compensated by the return of benefits as well as by the actual consciousness of the good deed. Remembrance of the love and good will of those whom you have benefited gives the mind a greater amount of pleasure than the bodily pleasure which you have forgone would have afforded. Finally—and religion easily brings this home to a mind which readily assents—God repays, in place of a brief and tiny pleasure, immense and never-ending gladness. (165–67)[13]

The reasoning involved in this argument recalls the generic conception of commonness invoked in the depreciation of gold and silver. True good, true pleasure, lies in the natural, and the example of mother nature shows that what is truly good and pleasant is always plentiful. True community does not derive from equal sharing of what is

13. That these pleasures are of the mind and spirit and not simply of the body is confirmed by the use of "gaudio" in the Latin. "In fact, theologically the term is almost reserved for the gladness of the beatific vision. The nature of the gladness is not fixed here but its description associates it with God, who alone can satisfy all man's yearnings" (*Utopia*, p. 451).

scarce, for scarcity will always lead to some manifestation of a utilitarian system of values; true community is founded on what each has in common and what is plentiful. And, if commonness is not natural to a commodity, as it is not with food or clothing, then each disciplines his own consciousness so as to make fulfillment derive from the happiness of a good conscience felt in the act of sharing these scarce goods. In both cases—natural and self-disciplined commonness—community is founded, as these examples show, upon a consciousness-in-conscience. The value of the humane gesture may derive from the "consciousness of the good deed," a form of graciousness. Or it may derive from a more religious consciousness, the awareness that God repays infinitely what man may give only finitely. Thus, nature truly understood leads man to find his rewards in his own self-awareness and understanding, characteristics common to all men.

Another corruption which may arise is a false conception of pleasure in the more temporal sense. One might tend to put corrupted pleasures before uncorrupted ones. Again, this false hierarchy grows out of a mistaken consciousness and is remedied by understanding the true character of nature's benevolence.

By pleasure they understand every movement and state of body or mind in which, under the guidance of nature, man delights to dwell. They are right in including man's natural inclinations. For just as the senses as well as right reason aim at whatever is pleasant by nature— whatever is not striven after through wrong-doing nor involves the loss of something more pleasant nor is followed by pain—so they hold that whatever things mortals imagine by a futile consensus to be sweet to them in spite of being against nature (as though they had the power to change the nature of things as they do their names) are all so far from making for happiness that they are even a great hindrance to it. (167)

True pleasure depends upon what nature benevolently and freely allows man to have without detriment to his fellow. Any other value system—even one which defines all good pleasures as those useful to the community—attacks and perverts nature and thus corrupts man's reason.

After suggesting that life's false pleasures are built upon customs which are man-made "since there is nothing sweet in them by nature" (171), More presents the genuine pleasures.

The pleasures which they admit as genuine they divide into various classes, some pleasures being attributed to the soul and others to the body. To the soul they ascribe intelligence and the sweetness which is bred of contemplation of truth. To these two are joined the pleasant recollection of a well-spent life and the sure hope of happiness to come.

Bodily pleasure they divide into two kinds. The first is that which fills the sense with clearly perceptible sweetness. Sometimes it comes from the renewal of those organs which have been weakened by our natural heat. . . .

The second kind of bodily pleasure they claim to be that which consists in a calm and harmonious state of the body. This is nothing else than each man's health undisturbed by any disorder. (173)

These genuine pleasures share two qualities. In the first place they reinforce man's sense of community by being based upon factors all may share in common without impinging upon the possession of them by another. Often this sense of commonness derives from the personal self-awareness which is the goal of nature and reason.

To sum up, they cling above all to mental pleasures, which they value as the first and foremost of all pleasures. Of these the principal part they hold to arise from the practice of the virtues and the consciousness of a good life. (175)

Secondly, especially in pleasures like good health, they reflect a cooperation with nature. Man builds genuine happiness not only from a unique form of commonness which allows complete sharing of infinite goods; he builds it also by enhancing rather than perverting mother nature.

Yet they enjoy even these pleasures and gratefully acknowledge the kindness of mother nature who, with alluring sweetness, coaxes her offspring to that which of necessity they must constantly do. (177)

Any other effort to attain pleasure or virtue, pursued for any other reason, however apparently noble, the Utopians and More find the extreme of madness.

This discussion of the Utopian ethic of pleasure, then, provides the means by which More and the reader may sort out the constructive ideals in Hythlodaeus' vision from the illusions that have come to dominate his mind. Moreover, this discussion has demonstrated the consistency between More's stance in Book I and the parerga and his implicit posture toward this Utopian creed. In all three of these phases of *Utopia* More affirms that the true drama of this life must be played out upon the stage of the individual's consciousness-in-conscience. Only here may man assert his right to govern his actions. Only here may man act out the play in hand yet remain free to judge his role. Each individual's consciousness-in-conscience, which enables him to look both out upon the experiences of man and in upon the dictates of his own mind, is the one and only vehicle which may transport man toward ideals that are free of any illusions or self-deceptions. In a similar manner, Hythlodaeus' rejection of this Utopian value system demonstrates the consistency of his posture in *Utopia* and reveals the source of his erring judgment. Focusing on the institutional patterns of this island people, preoccupied with the forms of their society alone, Raphael has created an illusory, false reality. The model which he sought to praise in his narrative has presented only the appearance of a "best state." Raphael has exchanged an illusion for an ideal and, in the process, has blinded himself to the obligations of his humanity. His *telos* seeks neither to secure a willing, universal agreement nor a true state of perfection. Rather, Hythlodaeus' Utopia only desires to preserve the illusion of its perfection intact. The persisting ambiguity of Raphael's vision—the place of the individual in this institutional hierarchy—has been dissipated; his illusion collapses because of its own self-created vacuum —the absence of the individual consciousness-in-conscience. The task left to the mediating poet and the detached reader is to discover the true ideals embodied in this utopian vision and to fix them firmly in the regions of the mind vacated by the collapse of Raphael's myth of perfection.

The investigation anticipated in More's objections to community of property at the close of Book I—an examination of how the individual may define himself and his relation to others in order to avoid the corrupting temptations of his nature—has now been completed in the discussion of Utopian ethics. The function of their union of virtue and pleasure in an integrated yet personal ethical code is to provide a means by which the individual, conscious of the demands of his own conscience as well as of the demands of his communal responsibilities, may aspire to a common agreement founded upon choice and reciprocity. This view of the human personality, associated in the text with the mediating poet, Thomas More, contrasts with Hythlodaeus' loss of all humanness and individuality in his consuming identification with the idealism of Utopian institutions. In the concluding sections of *Utopia*— "Slavery," "Military Affairs," and "Utopian Religions"— these two perspectives confront each other. In the section entitled "Slavery," Utopian institutions are again reviewed in a limbo of suspended judgment, for Hythlodaeus' willingness to leap over the individual conscience in order to proceed directly to the institutional ideal is checked by the reader's familiarity with the institutions discussed and his awareness of the role of the individual in them. This balancing of the institutional against the individual perspective in Utopian manners and customs, however, differs from the balance struck in the initial journey through Utopia, for now the contrast is systematized. Hythlodaeus is constantly urging the Utopian custom on More as a convenience to the Utopian society, an easy solution to a complex problem; More, on the other hand, is continually urging, implicitly, the reader to consider the custom in the light of the Utopians' consciousness-in-conscience reflected in their ethical creed and in the light of his own awareness of the personality's place in the institutional matrix of society.

With "Military Affairs" the balance can no longer be maintained. Hythlodaeus forces everything into compliance with his desire to preserve his idealism, and he leaves no room in his preoccupation with an illusory perfection for the poet to bring the actions described into a favorable relationship with reality. The apotheosis of Utopian idealism ends in the ironic destruction of the means the Utopians originally defined to guide their conduct—the family, a humanistic education, a sound ethical conscience. When all is subordinated to the unilateral thrust of rational coherence, there is no room left for the mediating consciousness-in-conscience to bring the ideal back to the existential context which gave birth to the wish for rational conduct. All problems are simplified to the one solution for preserving the ideal, and the irony becomes not simply that Hythlodaeus can see nothing except his rationalized social theory but also that his initial desire to rationalize human conduct destroys itself by the ease, the convenience, the efficiency with which his purpose is accomplished.

"Utopian Religions" returns More and the reader to the realm of the conscience. Indeed, since the institutional form alone has proved itself vacuous, the scale seems to shift almost too violently to the individual conscience. It becomes difficult to find any life-giving quality in the flabby formalities of Utopian worship. The institutions which struggled so violently for total supremacy in Utopian war policies now begin to slink powerless from the stage, much as Raphael, greatly weakened, must be led from the garden of his Discourse (245). The lesson of *Utopia* is that the return to Europe and reality means a return to the institutions and familiar traditions of everyday life; all that may be brought back from the Nowhere of the mind is the self-understanding which the experience has wrought in the individual mind. The human personality lost in Utopian military practices is finally and fully recovered.

The entrance into this loss-and-recovery of the indi-

vidual conscience commences in the relatively neutral
atmosphere of the section on "Slavery." In Utopia, slavery
replaces death as a penalty because through this manner
of punishment certain necessary social functions are performed—like butchering—which the Utopians consider
below their dignity. Not only does this slavery entail re-
pressing some segment of humanity, thereby revealing the
coercive potential of the Utopian ideal; it also isolates the
Utopian, shelters him from the trials of character which
engender a steeled self-discipline. The efforts of the Utopians to perpetuate a fugitive virtue suggest, in a subtle
way, the preference for an easy path to the common welfare rather than for one more difficult because it seeks to
preserve a concern for each individual's benefit. For, in
Utopia, the individual ends by placing his person in the
hands of the community, becomes dependent upon its coercive arm for his preservation, and thus, ironically, becomes
merely a tool in the planned preservation of the common
interest as embodied in the state. The Utopian citizen is
made as womanish by this subordination as any attendant
was ever enfeebled by the "noble" practice of keeping retainers. Isolation and institutional idealism, therefore, lead
away from realizing the individual's potential and toward
the illusion of perfection embodied in a sanctified corporate security.

Slavery, however, has another function among the Utopians, one which justifies many of the curious practices
described in this section by allowing the reentrance of the
individual conscience, its struggles, and its choices.

Their own countrymen are dealt with more harshly,
since their conduct is regarded as all the more re-
grettable and deserving a more severe punishment as
an object lesson because, having had an excellent rear-

ing to a virtuous life, they still could not be restrained from crime. (185)

In other words, slavery may also be a means for aiding one's awareness that human dignity depends upon reasonable and responsible conduct. Most negative controls in Utopia are designed with a similar purpose in mind. Thus slavery may have two effects: it may be merely a coercive device for social utility, or it may operate as a moral imperative, a warning to the conscience. Slavery earns Hythlodaeus' approval because it perpetuates normative conduct and eliminates unpleasant extremes. To More, Hythlodaeus' attitude reveals how institutionalized ideals may take on values one would traditionally believe to be the possession of the human being as a unique personality. Only when the institution of slavery is seen merely as a symbol of errors punished does the intended ideal emerge. It is as a metaphor of self-discipline that More would understand slavery; as a physical fact it ironically reveals the ideal as merely an illusion of benefits.

The negative controls supporting marriage are based on the knowledge that otherwise "few will contract the tie of marriage, in which a whole life must be spent with one companion and all the troubles incidental to it must be patiently borne" (187). The ancillary institutions—display of the bride and groom, divorce for adultery, separation by mutual consent—function not only to preserve marriage as an institution but also to increase the potentialities for good inherent in happy unions. Their effect is not so much to undercut the human personality as to create an atmosphere which cooperates with the affections which should be found in marriage. Again, then, negative controls, when directed toward individual welfare rather than institutional preservation, establish the larger community by first guaranteeing the interests and benefits of each individual within that community. When the institution grows naturally out of man's aspirations and addresses itself to his benefit, then its discipline becomes self-defined and self-imposed rather than externally applied. The value of the institution should be measured not in its ability to rationalize life successfully but in its potential contribution to the enhancement of man's reasonable nature.

The entire section on laws reflects a careful consideration of the justification and purpose of law in human conduct. Laws are meant to be regulators of behavior. As such, law is a logical extension of more personal controls: "Husbands correct their wives, and parents their children, unless the offense is so serious that it is to the advantage of public morality to have it punished openly" (191). One negative conclusion may be drawn from conceiving the state as a single family—that behavior ought to be subject to universal approbation or condemnation. Both misconduct and praiseworthy behavior are turned to public advantage. The danger in this universality is that it tends to steal from the mind its self-governing function, replacing it with fear of public disapproval or the desire for public praise.

> Not merely do they discourage crime by punishment but they offer honors to invite men to virtue. Hence, to great men who have done conspicuous service to their country they set up in the market place statues to stand as a record of noble exploits and, at the same time, to have the glory of forefathers serve their descendants as a spur and stimulus to virtue. (193)

If a public review of behavior is only an invitation to virtue, if, that is, the initiative still lies with the individual, to that extent this custom is laudable. To the extent that it is a "spur," however, universal exposure becomes a means to mobilize persons for the service of the society by prodding their vainglory. To that extent the custom serves only the state and the ideal corrupts the individual.

The open affections of the Utopian family generally are conducive to praiseworthy innovations. Solicitation of votes and coercion are eliminated. "No official is haughty or formidable. They are called fathers and show that character. Honor is paid them willingly, as it should be, and is not exacted from the reluctant" (195). By this means the stigma often associated with authority is replaced by natural and willing obedience, and the official only undercuts his position by peremptory conduct. In the same manner the openness of Utopia leads to an equitable application of the law. To the Utopians the greatest virtue of the law should be simplicity.

> This policy follows from their reasoning that, since all laws are promulgated to remind every man of his duty, the more recondite interpretation reminds only very few (for there are few who can arrive at it) whereas the more simple and obvious sense of the laws is open to all. (195)

This simplifying of the law, as contrasted with dictatorially redefining the legal code, looks back to the traditional meaning of law in society. Law was intended to remind man of his social duties and rights. This goal is not achieved simply by creating rational laws. Rather, the legal tradition must be rationalized; it must be freed from litigious subtleties, so that the law can actually remind man of the right conduct as well as punish him for the wrong action. The difference in effect between creating rational laws and rationalizing the legal tradition may seem small

at first glance, but it is not. The distinction lies at the very
heart of the differences between Hythlodaeus and More.
Raphael, engaged in his social theory, assumes that philosophic wisdom can be the immediate possession of an individual, a Utopus. More recognizes that no man, however
wise and well-trained, can possess complete rational
knowledge. Reason is the common possession of human
nature and therefore manifests itself only through a tradition which spans generations of men. What the individual
reason can understand are the lessons of the traditions of
human nature. Thus, More's poetic wish, as contrasted
with Hythlodaeus' theoretical imperative, calls only for
rationalizing the traditions of human nature as reflected
in the law, a policy which meant for More simplifying the
law so that it could reassume its role as man's institutionalized social conscience rather than continuing as the cage
in which to trap the individual conscience. Raphael attempts to equate his philosophic conscience with the common cause; More recognizes that the individual conscience
cooperates with the common cause only through its consciousness of the traditions of the community.

Institutionalizing a philosophic conscience motivated
only by detached and theoretical reason crushes human
society and the human personality, as will be seen in the
Utopian military policies. The individual conscience struggling to realize consciously man's common heritage and
the natural ties of the human social tradition constructs
the only true community, as may be seen in the Utopian
attitude toward treaties.

Treaties which all other nations so often conclude
among themselves, break, and renew, they never make
with any nation. "What is the use of a treaty," they
ask, "as though nature of herself did not sufficiently

bind one man to another? If a person does not regard nature, do you suppose he will care anything about words?" (197)

The true brotherhood of men only becomes real when it grows naturally from each individual's conscience guided by reason and his conscious subordinating of political to natural traditions. This affirmation of the natural and individual origin of community between nations is confirmed through satire.

In Europe, however, and especially in those parts where the faith and religion of Christ prevails, the majesty of treaties is everywhere holy and inviolable, partly through the justice and goodness of kings, partly through the reverence and fear of the Sovereign Pontiffs. (197)

The respect of the papacy for the holy and inviolable character of treaties may be seen in the conduct of Julius II.

Plainly, a powerful monarchy [France] was going to be a worse neighbour than a recalcitrant republic [Venice] and, disregarding altogether his treaty with Louis, Julius determined to expel the ally whom he had himself invited.[14]

The self-serving character of European diplomacy was a widespread phenomenon as may be seen in the Anglo-French treaty of 1514.

14. J. D. Mackie, *The Earlier Tudors: 1485–1558* (Oxford, 1952), p. 271.

As an essay in *Realpolitik* the Anglo-French treaty is a masterpiece. A reluctant princess [Mary of England] contracted a loveless marriage [to Louis XII]; two treacherous monarchs, Maximilian and Ferdinand, were themselves deceived and their dreams of controlling Italy were brought to nothing; Charles of Castile was driven to accept comprehension in the Anglo-French treaty, and France, recently expelled from Italy, was able once more to threaten Milan.[15]

By this treaty Henry VIII deserted Ferdinand (who himself had been exploiting Henry's inexperience to Spain's benefit) and joined with France. Though committed to aid France in defense, Henry actually withdrew from Europe to focus his attention on Scotland, recently divorced from French aid. France, however, did not mind this minor violation of the treaty, for her concern was merely to free herself from the English threat in order to concentrate her energies more fully in the Italian arena. Both the French and the English acted in this case solely out of self-interest and were soon to find themselves facing each other again. This justice of convenience ruled in Europe's regal courts; the common people, on the other hand, were governed by a more binding law.

> In consequence men think either that all justice is only a plebeian and low virtue which is far below the majesty of kings or that there are at least two forms of it: the one which goes on foot and creeps on the ground, fit only for the common sort and bound by many chains so that it can never overstep its barriers; the other a virtue of kings, which, as it is more august than that of ordi-

15. Ibid., p. 285.

nary folk, is also far freer so that everything is permissible to it—except what it finds disagreeable. (199)

By emphasizing the "reasoning" of the Utopians rather than their institutions and their practice in foreign policy, More is able to relate this satiric indictment to constructive ideas which could be carried to Europe by its educators —the humanists.

But the Utopians, on the contrary, think that nobody who has done you no harm should be accounted an enemy, that the fellowship created by nature takes the place of a treaty, and that men are better and more firmly joined together by good will than by pacts, by spirit than by words. (199)

From this fellowship of nature and good will issue two courses. Hythlodaeus retreats back to the defense of the independent existence of Utopian practices, the unsullied preservation of the model to which he has become committed. More moves forward to his humanist audience whom he hopes will spread and activate the spirit which is his ideal. Hythlodaeus' defense of Utopian military practices reveals that he prefers the limited existence of the ideal in its uncorrupted and shining detachment. He refuses to take the risk of corruption entailed in allowing man to attempt to govern himself with the Utopian standard in mind rather than to be governed from Olympus by the ideal.

The Utopians go to war for only three reasons, says Hythlodaeus.

They do so only to protect their own territory or to drive an invading enemy out of their friends' lands or, in pity for a people oppressed by tyranny, to deliver them by

force of arms from the yoke and slavery of the tyrant, a
course prompted by human sympathy. (201)

Stated so simply these three provocations to war seem
justifiable. Self-defense clearly is a cause for fighting. The
logical first extension of this principle of self-defense is
defense of the Utopians' friends. The logical second extension is a simple messianism—their defense will be extended to all people oppressed. What is alarming in this
inexorable march of reason is the power which it appro-
priates to itself and the ease with which it tramples traditions underfoot. The Utopians become first prosecutor
against all other powers, then judge in their own suit, and
finally executor of their judgment. The reason which grew
into the ideal defense of human nature now turns on that
nature in its blitzkrieg to rationalize all of life.[16]

The irony of this relentless rationalism is that its justice
cuts the Gordian knot of political complexity almost by
caprice.

The Nephelogetic traders suffered a wrong, as they
thought, under pretence of law, but whether right or
wrong, it was avenged by a fierce war. . . . The troubles
upon troubles that arose were ended only by the en-
slavement and surrender of the Alaopolitans. Since the
Utopians were not fighting in their own interest, they
yielded them into the power of the Nephelogetes, a people who, when the Alaopolitans were prosperous, were
not in the least comparable to them. (201)

16. Perhaps the most ironic aspect of this destruction of all human
values in the military practices of the Utopians is that it was the chaos
wrought by war on European society which first attracted Hythlodaeus'
scathing condemnation (see, *Utopia*, p. 311). A lesser but still poignant
thrust of the irony of these practices lies in the comment they make on
European practices of the time (see Ibid., pp. 502–06).

It suffices merely to bring suit in this Utopian tribunal. Whenever the Utopian ideal seems threatened, however tenuously, past traditions must fall before the instrument of Utopian reason. Though right or wrong may be uncertainly apportioned, apportioned they must be, and the consequences follow hard upon the resolution. The "fellowship created by nature," in the light of this example, gains a new definition—fellowship to those created in the image of Utopian nature. "So severely do the Utopians punish wrong done to their friends, even in money matters —but not wrongs done to themselves" (201). Such a noble gesture, however, must be qualified; the Utopians place great store in their citizens if not in property.

> If a Utopian citizen, however, is wrongfully disabled or killed anywhere, whether the plot is due to the government or to a private citizen, they first ascertain the facts by an embassy and then, if the guilty persons are not surrendered, they cannot be appeased but forthwith declare war. If the guilty persons are surrendered, they are punished either with death or with enslavement. (203)

The Utopians must be judge in their own cases; the justice of another country is like the plebeian justice which creeps along on foot and is not fitting to the dignity of kings or Utopian citizens.

Their prosecution of war seems to follow logically from their definition of human nature. "They boast themselves as having acted with valor and heroism whenever their victory is such as no animal except man could have won, that is, by strength of intellect" (203). Considered as an isolated policy, this program seems highly defensible as appropriate to man's nature. The problem arises from the fact that the Utopian ideal was defined in philosophic isolation, and its declaration in fact, rather than its evolutionary growth throughout the dispersed human community, intimidates the nonbelievers. Indeed, the Utopian policy of war is merely an extension of the intimidation employed in their penal code to guarantee preservation of their uniform social ideal. Though the Utopians consider slavery or death a kindness to any of their citizens who might dare speak or act against their code, they find playing upon man's innate doubts in order to foster dissension praiseworthy when the community being destroyed is other than their own. Thus bounties and bribes are matters of course.

If this plan does not succeed, they sow the seeds of dissension broadcast and foster strife by leading a brother of the king or one of the noblemen to hope that he may obtain the throne. If internal strife dies down, then they stir up and involve the neighbors of their enemies by reviving some forgotten claims to dominion such as kings have always at their disposal. (205)

When one considers the history of Europe from about 1400 on he can hardly deny the boasts of the Utopians about the effectiveness of their policies, nor doubt that the Utopians' disfavor is death. But the very act of recalling this tumultuous background reveals the most alarming danger of an unqualified, institutional rationalism. In the early years of the reign of Henry VII the intriguers for his throne could always find some assistance on the continent among England's enemies. And, whenever Ferdinand felt Henry VIII's animosity toward France waning in those hectic first few years of Henry's reign, he could always reawaken it by making vague hints about Henry's claim to the French throne.

Thus, what begins as the ideal hope of man, when turned toward its own defense rather than the defense of the interests of humanity, becomes the most insidiously self-serving of all policies. Hythlodaeus' philosophic idealism postulates its own correctness. That Utopian institutions are rational becomes more important than whether they serve all of humanity's best interests. By imposing himself between Raphael and the reader, More upholds the integrity of the individual against Hythlodaeus' fanatical pursuit of an illusory perfection. The role of the fictional More as the audience in this monologue serves to remind the reader that the interests of the common welfare are important because they are agreed upon as common, not because they are decreed to be universal. Hythlodaeus' utopianism leads directly to the dystopias of the twentieth century because he refuses to take up the challenge of mediating between the present reality and the hoped for ideality. The philosopher's task may be to choose goals; it cannot be to impose them. The choice of the best life must be evolved through the gradual progress of reciprocal understanding within the community. As More attempts to perform his role in *Utopia* as the poet mediating between man and his ideals, he points to the only lasting lesson of utopianism—the utopian myth, to be useful, must be about the means by which one approaches the *telos,* not an effort to define that end itself.

If the reader searches to no avail for the fellowship of nature in the rational aspects of Utopian military policy, he is equally frustrated when the Utopians employ force. Their force—the Zapoletans—bears a striking resemblance to the Swiss mercenaries, a resemblance which has been noted so often as not to require detailed examination again. What is more interesting and truly alarming is the munificence with which the Utopians credit themselves

as they carelessly send wave after wave of these Zapoletans
to their death.

The Utopians do not care in the least how many Zapoletans they lose, thinking that they would be the greatest
benefactors to the human race if they could relieve the
world of all the dregs of this abominable and impious
people. (209)

The irony of this dismissal of the Zapoletans as the dregs
of humanity is that the Zapoletans' guilt extends to those
who encourage their depravity by exploiting their mer-
cenary instincts. Indeed, the Utopians, who are so enlightened, deserve even more rigorous censure than the
Zapoletans, for the Utopians supposedly can see the true
fellowship of nature. They could, of course, if they were
not blinded by their efforts to perpetuate their own common interest.

The irony in the Utopian exploitation of the Zapoletans
becomes even more incisive when one recalls their condemnation of hunting and butchering. "Even in the case
of brute beasts, this desire of looking on bloodshed, in
their estimation, either arises from a cruel disposition or
degenerates finally into cruelty through the constant practice of such brutal pleasure" (171). Thus, an attitude so
strongly supported when in consonance with their needs
is conveniently forgotten when it conflicts with them.

But Hythlodaeus' ideal does not confine its intimidation
to others; rather, it willingly coerces the Utopians themselves into a terrifying perversion of natural fellowship.

Each man is surrounded by his own children and relations by marriage and blood so that those may be closest
and lend one another mutual assistance whom nature

most impels to help one another. It is the greatest re-
proach for a husband to return without his wife or for
a son to come back having lost his father. . . . The absence of anxiety about livelihood at home, as well as
the removal of that worry which troubles men about the
future of their families (for such solicitude everywhere
breaks the highest courage), makes their spirit exalted
and disdainful of defeat.

Moreover, their expert training in military discipline
gives them confidence. Finally, their good and sound
opinions, in which they have been trained from child-
hood both by teaching and by the good institutions of
their country, give them additional courage. $(211)^{17}$

Family affections do not exist for the benefit of the family's
members; they exist to enhance Utopia's ability to preserve

17. The praise which Hythlodaeus here bestows upon the "absence
of anxiety about livelihood at home" is very much consonant with his
own method of dealing with his family: "The possessions, which other
men do not resign unless they are old and sick . . . I divided among my
relatives and friends when I was not merely hale and hearty but actually
young" (55). Thus, both the Utopian example he praises and his own
attitude reduce the ties binding the family together to economic bonds, a
simplification which is as convenient for him (freeing him to philoso-
phize) as it is for the Utopian military. In direct contrast to this desire
to make life at home convenient is the example of Thomas More's
household (see Thomas Stapleton, *The Life and Illustrious Martyrdom
of Sir Thomas More*, tr. Philip E. Hallett [London, 1928], pp. 94–108).
More also affirms his deep emotional and intellectual commitment to his
family and suggests that this profound attachment should be the norm
in his letter to Peter Giles: "Besides, one must take care to be as agreeable as possible to those whom nature has supplied, or chance has
made, or you yourself have chosen, to be the companions of your life,
provided you do not spoil them by kindness, or through indulgence
make masters out of your servants" (39–41). Though this evidence is,
in part, indirect, the conclusion that the conduct Hythlodaeus here
finds so praiseworthy More would utterly and completely condemn
as inhuman is incontrovertible.

itself. Hythlodaeus praises community of property here because, by eliminating solicitude for each person's interests, an irresistible corporate courage is created. Utopian education achieves its institutional apotheosis not in what it may do to fertilize each man's nature and reason but in what it may do to compartmentalize personalities into an efficient war machine. After such a catalogue one can hardly doubt the invincibility of the Utopians, for, taken as a system to direct effort unilaterally, their society perverts the finest of their innovations—the reliance on family affections and authority meant to create respect for order, the shared responsibilities of the community meant to create a true brotherhood, the education and training in virtue meant to create the consciousness of the values of reason-in-conscience.

The destruction manifested above is the result of a misdirected application of the Utopian ideal to life. When the ideal takes its value from the life given it by each individual mind, it may become a constructive guiding principle. When Plato's *Republic*, for example, is understood as an analogy between the state and the wise man's mind, the coercion of the state becomes that disciplined wisdom of the mind which ultimately frees the individual.[18] When the Utopian ideal is taken literally, however, when the Utopian commonwealth becomes a true state which must either conquer or die, the principles of self-discipline, reason, and nature which it enshrines become instruments of coercion and irrational and unnatural intimidation.

But note that the constitution and daily discipline of Plato's ideal commonwealth converge to a single end:

18. Frye, "Varieties of Literary Utopias," pp. 331–32.

fitness for making war. Nietzsche's observation that war is the health of the state applies in all its fullness to Plato's Republic, for only in war is such stringent authority and coercion temporarily tolerable.[19]

In other words, Hythlodaeus' ideal commonwealth, taken literally, attains its fullest and most natural expression in these very war policies which end in destroying the individuals they were meant to protect. The illusory nature of perfection in the Utopia Hythlodaeus praises is nowhere clearer. Though one cannot give up the search for the true communal principle because of this ironic self-condemnation of the Utopian commonwealth, one must realize that community spirit does not become the ideal by a retreat into Raphael's isolated world of rational social theory; it only becomes an ideal when passed through the agency of individual consciences conscious of their place in the traditions of men.

With the presentation of Utopian military practices Hythlodaeus has brought Thomas More and the reader to the nadir in the cycle of the loss-and-recovery of the individual personality. The military in Utopia has preempted all individual rights, stripped the human personality of its self-governing potential, and coerced the individual conscience into a sterile, numbing, and meaningless agreement with rational institutional idealism. The irony of Hythlodaeus' position is that he has so totally submerged his own being in his ideal utopian state that he has become oblivious to the loss of self entailed in prescribing radical and categorical institutional reform. He cannot

19. Mumford, "Utopia," p. 274.

see that his Utopian social model has concluded its rationalization of life by consuming the self-disciplined consciousness that is the means by which the Utopians originally achieved their common agreement and general welfare. The institutions which Hythlodaeus has praised become vacuous, impotent, without the consciousness-inconscience which frees man to aspire to a rational ideal. Utopian religious practices, by returning the focus to the individual mind (as in the section on Utopian ethics), directs the reader to the true value of the utopian myth—the means, not the ends, which it discloses. In this final section, the emphasis returns to the origins from which Thomas More drew his *Utopia*—the family merely as a family, discipline as self-applied restraint, the conscience as the inner spirit of man. Thus, the final section of *Utopia* returns the reader to More's suggested arena of the individual conscience and concludes by seconding the spirit of community he advocates.

Early in this section on religion the impact of Christianity upon the Utopians is discussed.

But after they had heard from us the name of Christ, His teaching, His character, His miracles, and the no less wonderful constancy of the many martyrs whose blood freely shed had drawn so many nations far and wide into their fellowship, you would not believe how readily disposed they, too, were to join it, whether through the rather mysterious inspiration of God or because they thought it nearest to that belief which has the widest prevalence among them. But I think that this factor, too, was of no small weight, that they had heard that His disciples' common way of life had been pleasing to Christ and that it is still in use among the truest societies of Christians. (217–19)

Though the two passages of scripture relevant to this "common way of life" (Acts 2:44–45, 4:32–35) do not mention the equal sharing of goods, in both cases there is an emphasis on a communion of spirit.[20] Moreover, historically this common way of life was simply a result of the disciples' primary task—to be missionaries of the faith. Such a task required traveling, and the nomadic life was conducive to limited ownership at best. In any case, the reference is to *communio* which "denotes in its primary sense . . . the sublime Good that holds together the society of the faithful."[21] Thus the common way of life refers to a spiritual tradition and not a material one, a continuity which acts upon and through the individual conscience.

Since the "truest societies of Christians" may well refer to monastic orders (such as the Carthusians), one again may muster circumstantial evidence showing that this reference supports Utopian community of property.

The poverty of the individual Carthusian, monk or lay brother, consisted not in lack of necessities for the body or for the intellect, but in the complete renunciation of proprietorship.[22]

Again, however, this communism is justified upon the basis of a prior communion of spirit. Like the common sharing of possessions among Christ's disciples, it is only one possible means to the deeper and more important goal of communion with God.

20. *Utopia*, p. 519.
21. Ibid., quoting Jungmann, *Mass*, tr. Brunner, 2, 275 n. I.
22. E. Margaret Thompson, *The Carthusian Order in England* (London, 1930), p. 121. The Carthusian Order is taken as the example of European monastic life not only because its reputation for piety and adherence to its Rule in the early sixteenth century was rightly deserved but also because Thomas More spent four years (1499–1503)

Holding, as they [the Carthusians] do, with other Christians, that prayer is a mighty engine for the good of mankind, to which no other force is comparable, they go forward to the view that prayer to be most efficacious should be offered so far as possible by men in nearest communion with God—the effectual fervent prayer which avails much being that of a righteous man. And this communion—here we come to their real standing ground—can only be secured in their opinion by those who separate themselves from the cares, pleasures, distractions of the world by living a life of isolation in close commune with God.[23]

Thus, community of property is a superficial and, as it were, a casual expression of the true community sought. What the Utopians must have seen, or at least what More would have wanted understood that they saw, in this common way of life is an expression of the personal communion of spirit with other men and with the divinity which is so fully expressed in the religious foundation of their ethics.

The Utopian system of toleration is also interesting for the light which it sheds upon the true sources of community.

Moreover, even if it should be the case that one single religion is true and all the rest are false, he [Utopus] foresaw that, provided the matter was handled reasonably and moderately, truth by its own natural force

---

in communication with the monks of the London Charterhouse, most probably as a lay brother (see William Roper, *The Lyfe of Sir Thomas Moore, Knighte,* ed. Elsie Vaughan Hitchcock [London, 1935], p. 6).

23. Gerald S. Davies, *Charterhouse in London* (London, 1921), p. 49.

would finally emerge sooner or later and stand forth
conspicuously. (221)

The assumption which underlies this toleration ("truth
by its own natural force would finally emerge") is that
which More reiterated against Luther: "natural reason
. . . is 'servant to faith, not enemy.' "[24] Therefore, reason
will eventually lead to the true faith, much as man's nature
inclines him toward gracious conduct. These two principles lead to that communion of spirit which grows out
of each individual's recognition of the humanity he shares
with his fellow. Though without Christianity this communion remains incomplete, Utopus' assumption is that
man tends naturally toward that brotherhood which Christ
founded upon Faith, Hope, and Charity.

To assure that no one should fall "below the dignity of
human nature" (221), however, Utopus outlined the principles of a minimal religion, the same principles from
which the Utopians draw their ethics.

By way of exception, he conscientiously and strictly
gave injunction that no one should fall so far below the
dignity of human nature as to believe that souls like-
wise perish with the body or that the world is the mere
sport of chance and not governed by any divine providence. After this life, accordingly, vices are ordained to
be punished and virtue rewarded. (221)

On these principles the Utopians not only construct the
consciousness of virtue which is the source of their pleasures; on them they also construct that consciousness of
obligation to gracious behavior which is the foundation

24. O'Sullivan, p. 51.

for respect of the law (223). The final and most real consciousness which develops from these principles is the living belief in an afterlife that continues the temporary communion of souls on earth.

> Consequently they believe that the dead move about among the living and are witnesses of their words and actions. Hence, they go about their business with more confidence because of reliance on such protection. The belief, moreover, in the personal presence of their forefathers keeps men from any secret dishonorable deed. (225)[25]

Through such principles the Utopian social community reflects More's own goal—the foundation of ideal conduct upon the individual consciousness-in-conscience and the willingly fulfilled personal obligation to the larger community, a community which is continuous not only between generations and among neighbors but even across life's threshold.

25. The importance of this belief as a means by which the Utopian individual hopes to guide his conduct toward the traditional humanistic and catholic goal of mutual love and charity is partially obscured in this translation. The emphasis on the spirit of Utopian practices (a spirit which would help to repair the absence of revealed religion in Utopia by demonstrating how natural religion may guide man toward divine truths) in Robynson's translation more clearly reveals how the belief in the liberation which must follow death functions as a guide to the individual Utopian conscience. "The modern translation tells us that this belief is sustained by the conjecture of the Utopians that freedom (of movement), like all other good things, must be increased for good men after death. The Tudor translator, Raphe Robynson, managed, though clumsily, rather better: though he broke up the sentence, he allowed himself to be guided in sense by its syntax and, without seriously sacrificing its *libertate,* arrived at the conclusion that the good dead are moved by *mutuus amor charitasque,* 'whyche in good men after theyre deathe they cownte to be rather encreased then

The strictness with which this social philosophy is bound to realizing the contemplative ideal in the active life is revealed in the transformation that is worked in Utopia on monasticism. The highest expression of the monastic ideal in Europe is contained in the creed of the Carthusians:

It is the life of contemplation and mysticism carried to the utmost. The Carthusian's aim, as stated by a modern member of the Order, is to begin on earth the life of contemplation, love, and praise of God that they look forward to as the sum of the heavenly life to follow.[26]

In the orders of the "true Religious" in Utopia, the Utopian equivalent of European monastic communities, the active life is both their act of privation itself and also, like good works in Catholicism, one of the goals of religion in this life.

There is special privation. There is the base labor to induce and foster a special humility. There is the special vocation, the religious calling. And finally there is the irrelevance of their existence to the social structure of the Utopian commonwealth.[27]

---

dymynyshede.' The 1517 version supports Robynson against Richards [the translation, with some changes by Surtz, of this edition], though his antecedent is perhaps still somewhat unnecessarily uncertain; for 1517 clearly implies that it is *charitas* which is increased in the good dead, and the rest follows from that. As Father Surtz's quotations in an explanatory note indicate (531), this is not a doctrinal crux" (Arthur E. Barker, "Review Article: Clavis Moreana: The Yale Edition of Thomas More," *Journal of English and Germanic Philology,* 65 [April 1966], 326).

26. William F. Taylor, *The Charterhouse of London* (London, 1912), p. 27.

27. Hexter, p. 90.

These orders may be irrelevant to the Utopian society in the sense that they are unnecessary to it. But their commitment to unsolicited social activity ("While perpetually engaged in hard work themselves, they secure leisure for the others and yet claim no credit for it"[225–27]) expresses the aspirations of Utopian society in the same manner as the contemplative goals of the monastic orders expressed the aspirations of the early Christian culture from which they grew.

The conduct of the Utopian "Buthrescae" (227) underlines as deeply as possible the relevance of voluntary charitable conduct to the full realization of the human personality in the earthly communion that is the true Utopian ideal. The Utopian priests express the nature of their pastoral vocation not only in their "extraordinary holiness" (227) but also in their role in the formal education of the young. In Utopia education is a continuing and pervasive phenomenon, perpetuated in all family gatherings as well as in formal courses for adults long after they have joined the active community. Strictly formal education, however, is entrusted to the priesthood in order to develop the relationship between virtue and the proper exercise of reason most clearly.

To the priests is entrusted the education of children and youths. They regard concern for their morals and virtue as no less important than for their advancement in learning. They take the greatest pains from the very first to instill into children's minds, while still tender and pliable, good opinions which are also useful for the preservation of their commonwealth. When once they are firmly implanted in children, they accompany them all through their adult lives and are of great help in watching over the condition of the commonwealth.

The latter never decays except through vices which arise from wrong attitudes. (229)

Thus, the links between right reason, consciousness-in-conscience, and the religious traditions of true community are forged more completely. The priesthood, as the balance to the executive arm of the commonwealth, not only acts as a counterweight to its authority but also functions as its partner in the greater goal of realizing, as far as possible within the limits of human nature, the heavenly communion of souls in the earthly brotherhood and fellowship of men.

Moreover, the family returns to the forefront as an institution of open affection, willing self-discipline, and the origin of the consciousness of a good conscience.

On the Final-Feasts, before they go to the temple, wives fall down at the feet of their husbands, children at the feet of their parents. They confess that they have erred, either by committing some fault or by performing some duty carelessly, and beg pardon for their offense. Hence, if any cloud of quarrel in the family has arisen, it is dispelled by this satisfaction so that with pure and clear minds they may be present at the sacrifices, for it is sacrilegious to attend with a troubled conscience. (233)

This is not the novel family structure tied to the system of a rotating communal farm population which was necessitated by Hythlodaeus' ideal of community of property. Rather, it is the family familiar to Thomas More, reverent, close-knit, nurturing a religious conscience, disciplined merrily by a willing submission to proper authority.[28] In-

28. Cf. Stapleton, pp. 94–108.

deed, the institution of the family is not what is important any longer; much like the community the Utopians saw in early Christianity, the institutional ideal is only a casual expression of what is really being emphasized. The important quality of this Utopian family is the spirit of brotherhood which it expresses, the harmony which exists between the traditions of familial organization and the intentions and conduct of the members of the family. More, contrary to Plato's example, has placed the family at the center of the true Utopian ideal because there is no novelty in the institution, because the essence of the Utopian ideal is the self-disciplined consciousness-in-conscience which seeks expression in the traditional patterns and the familiar rituals of life.

This is nowhere clearer than in the treatment given to Utopian forms of worship. Utopian religious practices and methods of worship are guided by two principles. One is that nothing should be included "which does not seem to agree with all in common" (233). In this way, the institution, by virtue of its generality, is stripped of any significance in itself; it becomes indistinct and undistinctive. The other principle is that the Utopians include in their worship many practices such as burning incense, candles, and other fragrant substances (235). They consider that these practices are harmless in themselves, and that they seem to lead the mind to God. This kind of "utility" contrasts strongly with that social utility which finally perverts Hythlodaeus' ideal, since this utility depends for its strength upon the individual mind and will. In other words, many features of the Utopian system of worship are not essential to any institutional ideal; their value depends upon the spiritual endowment provided by each individual's religious conscience.

The description of "Utopian Religions" closes by presenting their form of common prayer. In this prayer the Utopians give thanks for their blessings and ask that God's will—whether it sanction their form of life or another—may be realized through them as He wishes (237). The seeming flabbiness of this prayer becomes a form of strength when placed in the context of the Utopian ideal that I have described, for the purpose of this generality is "that each individual may apply to himself *personally* what all recite together" (237—italics mine).[29] The very banality of the institutional form reveals that the source of the true Utopian idealism is not in the images the iconoclastic Hythlodaeus seeks to praise but in the spirit which generates those forms, the means by which they are brought to life and given an existential content. Thus, as the Utopian narrative closes, the reader is confronted with a lifeless institutionalism on the one hand (either destroying the individual as in Utopian military practices or being vague, flabby, and nonessential as in Utopian religious practices) and the spirit of the disciplined con-

29. The distinction emphasized by the italics is justified by the Latin where "priuatim" is contrasted with "cuncti" (236)—the whole group. A similar contrast between a generalized public form and the meaning given it by the private conscience occurs in the Latin text on p. 232: "publica tali peragunt ordine, qui nulli prorsus ex priuatis deroget." Unfortunately, this sentence was omitted in the translation. Clarence Miller has supplied an accurate English rendering of the Latin: "Public worship is conducted according to a ritual which does not at all detract from any of the private devotions" (Miller, p. 59). Sylvester has confirmed the placement of this translation in the text of the Yale edition (233/11—after "home" and before "Therefore"). With both of these contrasts between the public form and the private meaning the point is the same: the institution is superfluous; what counts is the manner in which each conscience adjusts its relation to the divine within the unimportant format. Hythlodaeus' institutional idealism is thus completely deflated here, and the emphasis clearly rests with More's focus upon Utopia as a myth disclosing means by which to guide human conduct, not ends demanding universal allegiance.

science aware of its relation to itself, to its immediate environment, and ultimately to the spiritual meaning of God Himself on the other. Hythlodaeus' idealism has prompted the journey to Utopia, but his immersion in the institutional significance of the Utopian commonwealth has blinded him to the true community to be discovered there. More was engaged by Raphael's visionary ability but was able to remain detached from the illusory in his idealism, was able to return to Europe, was able to mediate between man's rational hopes and his traditional rituals.

# 4

## Thomas More's *Utopia*:
## A Myth of Means

No analysis of *Utopia* can ever hope to encompass the full meaning of the work. A reader's final inability to delineate in one explanation the statement made by a work of art is the very definition of good literature, and More's *Utopia* is definitely good literature. Inevitably much of the richness of More's masterpiece does not emerge in this essay, which tries to focus exclusively upon one of the principal thematic issues in the work—the role of social myth or utopian idealism in the real world. My choice of this focal point to some extent derives from the fact that in wrestling with the problems of man in society Thomas More faces most squarely problems relevant to us now. But this choice also rests upon the firm conviction that Thomas More intended to deal first and foremost with man as a social animal. What makes *Utopia* difficult to analyze is that More does not structure his arguments around issues; he does not state his purpose and then proceed to prove his point of view explicitly. Rather, his analysis of man's role in culture proceeds implicitly and, to some extent, disjointedly. Indeed, much of his method is negative: the dialogues of Book I and the irony in the monologic Discourse of Book II often seem to reveal only what is false, illusory, or misleading in any given perspec-

tive, especially in a perspective grounded in the easy institutionalism of community of property or the efficient
rationalism of coherent social theories. The positive statement, the affirmative expression of truth, always seems to
elude the reader's grasp. The recognition that *Utopia* is
fantasy and not rational theory, for example, implies that
social truths are not easy and simple but complex and
open-ended. One is finally left with the feeling that this
fantastic and open-ended quality of *Utopia* is not merely
a convention, but that More employs this evolving and
dialogic movement in order to say that truth itself is
elusive. In other words, the fantasy and open-endedness
of *Utopia* come to have a substantive meaning: ultimately
More's utopian myth is not about the ends to which life
should be directed but about the means man should employ to achieve ends which have been predetermined, as
much as they can be, by God and human nature.

That Utopia is open-ended, that it closes with an invitation to further dialogue, is obvious in its last lines.

> I therefore praised their way of life and his speech and,
> taking him by the hand, led him in to supper. I first said,
> nevertheless, that there would be another chance to
> think about these matters more deeply and to talk them
> over with him more fully. If only this were some day
> possible! (245)

The exclamatory sentence offers the challenge. The reader
has Hythlodaeus before him, his ideals laid out for examination. He need only begin. The temporal suggestion,
however, also reflects a concern for stimulating action
along with debate. It introduces an ambiguity which More
finally leaves to the reader: the day for realizing these
utopian ideals never quite seems to come:

But I readily admit that there are very many features in the Utopian commonwealth which it is easier for me to wish for in our countries than to have any hope of seeing realized. (245–47)

This temporal gap between achievement and what is hoped for becomes More's challenge to the reader. It is not merely that the wish for a utopian ideal must precede the fact and is easier to engender than actually to attain in life; it is that the wish, the aspiring will to act, is the final bridge between Utopia and Europe. Utopia is not a place but a Nowhere; it is a point in the mind, not an epoch in history. Mythological presentations of the utopian *telos* must always locate the ideal temporally or spatially; but myth is simply the activating, the setting in motion, of the word. Utopia comes to man in words; it remains beyond man in actions. Thus, the real invitation with which *Utopia* closes is twofold: on the one hand, More invites men to further discussion in order to make more precise what the utopian myth of means really should be; on the other hand, he urges men not merely to debate but to hope and to begin to pursue their hopes. When Utopia crosses over the threshold of the mind into the active life, the open-ended discussion achieves a substantive meaning: the struggle of words becomes also a struggle of deeds.

How much More's method in *Utopia* proceeds implicitly, how much it leads away from final statements of institutional ideals and toward focusing on the means by which man should guide his life, is nowhere more clearly revealed than when the posture of defending an absolute statement is assumed. There are three consciously undertaken "defenses" in *Utopia:* in the first phase of the work—the parerga—More presents a "defense" of his work; in the second phase—the dialogue of Book I—

he presents a "defense" of private property; in response
to this Hythlodaeus undertakes a "defense" of community
of property which becomes the focus of the third phase of
the work—the Discourse of Book II. Each of these "defenses" ends in a qualification which is intended to push
the reader beyond the closed implications of a final statement of absolute fact to an open-ended investigation of the
means which individuals should employ in adapting themselves to the suggestive outlines of an ultimate goal.

More's "defense" of *Utopia* was expressed in his letter
to Peter Giles. He is speaking of the comments made by a
critic of his work:

> Why should he be so minded [as to think himself "sharp-
> sighted"] as if there were nothing absurd elsewhere in
> the world or as if any of all the philosophers had ever
> ordered the commonwealth, the ruler, or even the pri-
> vate home without instituting some feature that had
> better be changed? (249)

On the surface this reply reads as a "defense" of some of
the inconsistencies in Hythlodaeus' Utopian image. But
the argument can be turned around to condemn Utopia
as an institutional ideal, since it states explicitly that no
man, however wise, can hope to define a social goal that
may legitimately claim every man's allegiance. In other
words, this "defense" of *Utopia* becomes a true defense
only if one understands that by it More is pushing the
reader beyond Hythlodaeus' incarnated rational ideal to a
state of consciousness which transforms the state of Utopia
into a metaphor of each individual's adjustment of his
social ideals to the world of social tradition—an adjustment that can take place only in a consciousness guided
by good conscience.

The second "defense" is More's presentation, at the end of the Dialogue of Counsel, of the traditional objections of an ownership society to communism. This places his "defense" of private property against Hythlodaeus' "defense" of community of property. Such a juxtaposition would seem to imply that one position will eventually triumph over the other. The dynamics of this confrontation, however, are not so simple or unidirectional. The ambiguity of these "defenses" is reflected in the closing words of *Utopia* when their arguments are reviewed. Hexter is correct in observing that More places the weaker of his two "defenses" of private property in the climactic position and, by doing so, seems to dissociate himself from the practices of European ownership.

> Now if anyone honestly wanted to uphold private property, surely he would rest his case with a mature, not with a palpably silly and insincere, argument. More does the opposite. Against Hythloday's magnificent invective hurled at private property at the end of Book II, he sets not the serious but the silly defense of it. This juxtaposition at the very end of the published version of *Utopia* leaves the reader with a feeling of disgust at the evils of private property. This is precisely the effect that anyone in his good senses would expect from such an ending, and More was certainly in his good senses when he wrote it.[1]

Hexter is absolutely correct in saying that the rhetoric of these two arguments leaves the reader disgusted with the corrupting effects of private property as seen in European practice. He is also correct in arguing that More must have intended by this to push beyond a simple defense of ownership, of meum and tuum, in contemporary Europe. He

---

1. Hexter, *Utopia: The Biography,* p. 39.

overstates his case, however, when he concludes that the weak arguments of the "final defense" of private property imply that the traditional and cogent "defense" placed just before the opening of the Discourse was merely "a straw man that he had already not only knocked down but utterly and completely demolished."[2] Private ownership does not emerge from *Utopia* untarnished; but a cursory review of the ironic undercutting of community of property reveals that that institution, too, is condemned in some of its applications.

More's objections to community of property at the end of Book I serve to establish the true focus of reform: social corruption, though it is reflected in the manner in which man uses his institutions, begins with the wickedness inherent in human nature. Thus, when Hythlodaeus defends the ability of community of property to root out this evil, his perspective becomes one-sided: his "defense" becomes ironic in the ease, the facility, the efficiency, which characterize his radical communistic solution:

> In Utopia all greed for money was entirely removed with the use of money. What a mass of troubles was then cut away! What a crop of crimes was then pulled up by the roots! Who does not know that fraud, theft, rapine, quarrels, disorders, brawls, seditions, murders, treasons, poisonings, which are avenged rather than restrained by daily executions, die out with the destruction of money? Who does not know that fear, anxiety, worries, toils, and sleepless nights will also perish at the same time as money? (241–43)

Hythlodaeus, in the debate about thievery at Cardinal Morton's, has amply demonstrated the vengeful character of contemporary social justice in England. But the irony

2. Ibid., p. 42.

is that Hythlodaeus has really not attacked the roots of
corruption through his Utopian communism; all that he
has done is focus his vengeance on taking money rather
than on possessing it. The images of dissecting, of rooting
up, of plucking out, are important in their ironic impact.
They are the same images Hythlodaeus used when attacking the injustice of ownership in England. The violence of
these images reflects, in both cases, the efficiency of the
institutions, not their fairness. The rhetorical force of his
question—"who does not know?"—turns upon him. While
he was the one who knew how unfair were the methods of
justice in England's social structure, he is the only one who
does not realize the devastations wrought by his own idealism. It has consumed his own insights, his own personality,
his own sense of responsibility to his family, his citizenship and sense of community, just as it consumes all the
potential in the human personality in its blitzkrieg assault
on the wickedness of corrupted humanity. The efficiency
of his rational and institutional idealism takes away the
struggle of being a man, the difficulties which give any
gain its preciousness. What it substitutes for the image of
free man striving for constructive self-realization is not
happy perfection and merry discipline but permanent oppression, the coercion of violent, self-preserving idealism:

> At home they have extirpated the roots of ambition and
> factionalism along with all other vices. Hence there is
> no danger of trouble from domestic discord, which has
> been the only cause of ruin to the well-established pros-
> perity of many cities. As long as harmony is preserved
> at home and its institutions are in a healthy state, not
> all the envy of neighboring rulers, though it has rather
> often attempted it and has always been repelled, can
> avail to shatter or to shake that nation. (245)

There can be no doubt that community of property, reinforced by the institutional discipline necessary to maintain it as an ideal, can eliminate manifestations of corruption. But the price is violence to the human being, a violence reflected vividly in Hythlodaeus' bellicose language and truculent "defense." And the error involved in seeing community of property as the ideal solution to the problems besetting man is that Hythlodaeus' communism, reinforced by institutional coercion, only eliminates the *manifestations* of corruption, not the *sources* of human wickedness. His "defense" is accurate to the extent that one can accept an institutional rooting out of corruption as a final solution to the human dilemma; but his "defense" ironically reveals itself as a false and illusory solution in its radical violence as well as in the ease with which it attains its end by glossing over the complexity of the human personality.

If, in *Utopia,* More is defending neither private property nor community of property, then what is he defending? The answer is quite clear. It is expressed in the Utopian system of ethics. More is defending a community spirit, a feeling of brotherhood which may be found in either the ideals of private property or the ideals of community of property. He is defending not an institutionalized end but an individualized means: the reciprocal freedom which builds man's feeling of community upon the sense of personal and willingly fulfilled obligation to one's fellow that comes from the recognition of human nature's commonness—a common inheritance, common possessions, and a common destiny for all men. Thus, it is very sensible that the serious objections to community of property precede the Discourse. Their purpose is to push the mind dialogically past the institutional manifestations of community to the spirit of brotherhood, commonness, and consciousness-in-conscience from which the only true community may grow. It is equally sensible that the ironic defense of private property follows Hythlodaeus' eulogy of community of property, for the irony turned upon ownership, coupled with More's personally expressed doubts about institutional communism, confirms the reader's conviction that true community is spiritual, not institutional.

The full text of this concluding evaluation by the author reveals that More is really dismissing the very notion of institutional perfection.

> When Raphael had finished his story, many things came to my mind which seemed very absurdly established in the customs and laws of the people described—not only in their method of waging war, their ceremonies and religion, as well as their other institutions, but most of all in that feature which is the principal foundation of their whole structure. I mean their common life and subsistence—without any exchange of money. This latter alone utterly overthrows all the nobility, magnificence, splendor, and majesty which are, in the estimation of the common people, the true glories and ornaments of the commonwealth. (245)

Clearly, this "estimation of the common people," which sees the glory of the commonwealth in superfluous display, represents an utterly demolished and nonsensical position. But what of the objections raised in a serious tone in the beginning of this passage? The Utopian method of waging war has ironically revealed itself as the complete perversion of whatever was well-established in the Utopian scheme of things. Similarly, Utopian ceremonies, taken merely as institutions, proved banal. And if one understands by this reference to religion not the principles or spiritual underpinnings of Utopian religious practices but some of these practices themselves, one may see that these institutions too are ironically inconsistent.

> They mock at auguries and divinations which are admired in other countries; yet they pray publicly for miracles and look confidently for the fulfillment of their prayers. [see 225] And they would have departed from superstition had not "an untoward event, which chance brought upon one of their number when he was deliberating on a change of religion, been construed by fear as not having happened by chance but as having been sent from heaven."[3] [see 217]

What, then, is being dismissed is the *literal* and *factual* impact of *Utopia,* just as the ironic praise of European splendor in ownership dismisses the practices often accompanying private property without necessarily disparaging the charitable spirit that ownership may prompt. If one were to take Hythlodaeus' institutional arguments literally, the praise of these novelties would be as ironic as More's praise of the European use of private property. The condemnation here is not simply of private property but of

---

3. Ward Allen, "Speculations on St. Thomas More's Use of Hesychius," *Philological Quarterly, 46* (April 1967), 159. The English translation, by focusing upon one event occurring to one individual while he was "deliberating on a change of religion," does not fully bring out the corruption of the individual conscience by a too-willing reliance upon seemingly convincing formal patterns which this passage portrays, for, as Clarence Miller notes, the "Utopians are actually not so impressionable that one episode could preserve superstition among them for a long time. What the Latin says is 'had not whatever untoward event that happened to anyone when he was deliberating etc' " (Miller, "The English Translation," p. 61). This more literal translation reveals the more general character of the phenomenon of institutions undercutting the potential God has endowed in each individual conscience to seek out truth and emphasizes how an idealism of forms impoverishes the consciousness of good which is man's true path toward the ideal.

all subordinations of the individual to the institutional ideal. What More is here confirming is the same message he has confirmed throughout *Utopia:* that *his* utopian ideal proceeds from the ends to the means, from the institution to the individual and finally to the personal consciousness-in-conscience of human fellowship. It is this personal consciousness which transforms the ideal of the mind, the fantastic goal of the fiction, into the world of action. This consciousness is necessary to confirm that all aspiring toward the ideal *must* begin in the play in hand. Beyond this, however, consciousness-in-conscience becomes the means to the ideal because it not only can recognize the actual historical traditions which entrap man but also can perceive the traditions of uncorrupted human nature to which man should aspire. More's ideals are really ideals for each individual within society. The courage of *Utopia* is manifested as More faces the fact that perfection is not the result of fiat but of long, gradual, and arduous personal struggles, for only in self-disciplined reciprocal freedom may individuals find the permanent roots of the true common interest.

This consciousness-in-conscience, then, first of all founds the community upon what is truly common to all—the benevolent gifts of nature like earth, water, and air, the potentialities of human nature and reason, the shared destiny of a future life of rewards for virtue and punishment for vices, and the infinite consciousness of the good deed done in right conscience. And if goods are by their nature limited—such as food, shelter, and clothing—the Utopians discipline themselves to find the "natural" value of these scarce items in the consciousness of the good bestowed on both the giver and the receiver in the act of willing, charitable sharing. Moreover, this self-discipline has another liberating effect. By founding all worth in one's conscience and consciousness, one eliminates his subjection to the caprices of material fortunes. More has expressed this attitude in the discussion of the Utopian Epicurean-Stoic ethic. The key to the efficacy of this ethic lies in its recognition of the difficulty of maintaining such an attitude—an insight confirmed by focusing on means and not ends in that discussion. A similar focus may be seen in More's early poems on fortune:

### Thomas More to them that trust in fortune

Thou that art prowde of honour shape or kynne.
That hepest up this wretched worldes treasure,
Thy fingers shrined with gold, thy tawny skynne,
With fresh apparayle garnished out of measure,
And wenest to have fortune at thy pleasure,
Cast up thyne eye, and loke how slipper [elusive, slippery] chaunce,
Illudeth [deceives] her men with chaunge and vary-aunce.

. . .

Wherefore yf thou in suretye lyst to stande,
Take poverties parte and let prowde fortune go,
Receyve nothyng that commeth from her hande:
Love maner [manners, i.e. moral excellence] and vertue: they be only tho [those].
Whiche double fortune may not take the fro.
Then mayst thou boldly defye her turnyng chaunce:
She can the neyther hynder nor avaunce.[4]

The lesson of both *Utopia* and this poem on fortune is at once simple and profound: man is truly free and secure

4. W. E. Campbell, *The English Works of Sir Thomas More* (London, 1931), pp. 339–43.

only when he rules his life by his own conscience and finds his values in his own consciousness rather than in the material signs of the mutable world.

Finally, the self-discipline of consciousness-in-conscience frees man from that inner corruption (pride) which hinders true communion.[5]

Pride measures prosperity not by her own advantages but by others' disadvantages. Pride would not consent to be made even a goddess if no poor wretches were left for her to domineer over and scoff at, if her good fortune might not dazzle by comparison with their miseries, if the display of her riches did not torment and intensify their poverty. This serpent from hell entwines itself around the hearts of men and acts like the suckfish in preventing and hindering them from entering on a better way of life. (243–45)

As with his poem on Fortune, More confirms here the difficulty and the individual character of the struggle against the corrupting forces working against man in society. But pride, because it is founded on invidious comparisons, becomes subject to the same caprices of fortune which beset misguided man. In placing oneself within the disciplined awareness of a consciousness-in-conscience one frees oneself from Fortune's Wheel and, at the same time, makes that wheel the rack upon which pride can be tortured to its death.

5. Thomas More, in the company of many others, confirms time and again the proverb that pride is the root of all evil (*Utopia*, p. 565). He gives life to this commonplace, however, by using it to anchor his entire analytical approach in *Utopia;* by it he confirms his inversion of Plato: bridging the gap between word and action, ideality and reality, progressing toward the ideal state can only be accomplished by reforming the individual consciousness-in-conscience.

Indeed, the contrast between More's ideal of consciousness-in-conscience and Hythlodaeus' deceiving and self-
destructive idealism is summarized most succinctly in
More's interlocking of three ideas—Fortune, the vision of
life as a play, and the meaning of tradition. They are joined
in a speech by Menippus in Lucian's *Necromantia*—a dialogue translated by More in 1506.[6]

> So as I [Menippus] looked at them [the dead] it seemed
> to me that human life is like a long pageant, and that all
> its trappings are supplied and distributed by Fortune,
> who arrays the participants in various costumes of many
> colours. . . . Some, however, are so ungrateful that when
> Fortune appears to them and asks her trappings back,
> they are vexed and indignant, as if they were being
> robbed of their own property, instead of giving back
> what they had borrowed for a little time.[7]

As More turned these ideas over in his mind and expressed
them in different works he explored the various implications of such a relationship to life. In their use in *Utopia*
he discovered that, though fortune may control certain
material traditions she cannot impair (or enhance) the
traditions nature gives to all men—the commonness of
reason and natural inclinations and the same destiny determined by the same judgment upon the use of these common possessions. Moreover, life must be played out according to the script at hand (whether it be Lucian's
tragedy[8] or Erasmus' comedy[9]); the actors in this drama

6. Dean, "Literary Problems," p. 32.
7. Lucian, *Necromantia, 4,* Loeb tr. A. M. Harmon (Cambridge,
Mass., 1961), pp. 99–101.
8. Ibid., p. 101.
9. Erasmus, *The Praise of Folly,* p. 38.

achieve their only true expression not in the eyes of other actors in the same play but only in their own consciousnesses of their roles in the act and scene. The only judge of their performance must be their consciousness of a role acted in good conscience. More recognizes, as Hythlodaeus cannot, that man is part of the world. He also recognizes, as Hythlodaeus does not, that man is not simply part of utopia. Utopia is translated into Europe not through institutions but through men like the Christian humanists who have experienced the ironies of the ideal as well as of the real and attempt to overcome both by struggling toward utopia without becoming subsumed in it and participating in the political world without being of it.

Thus, More attacks community of property from the vantage point of the ideals enshrined in the orthordox justifications of ownership (Catholic doctrine and the philosophy of the common law) not to affirm one or deny the other but to go beyond both to the underlying spirit of community. This fellowship of all men is built on the common and shared facts of life for all human beings, the consciousness of this natural human tradition, and the potential for gracious communion embodied in measuring life within the arena of the conscience. Only in this way may man really fulfill his own personal wishes while still serving the common interest; only when freedom is reciprocal, choice open to all, and community the expression of a personally-felt obligation does the utopian ideal of man's brotherhood become realizable in the active life as well as conceivable in the mind. Hythlodaeus, the prophet-philosopher-physician, envisioned this ideal as a coherent rational theory; Morton argued that the common interest can be expressed only in the world which allows to man the free play of his will; More bridges the gap between these two, between the contemplative and the active, between fiction and reality, by uniting these radical opposites in the individual consciousness-in-conscience. The Utopian ideal remains open-ended not only in the sense that no man or group of men may define the social goals which will command the allegiance of everyone but also in the more substantively dialogic sense, that progress toward the ideal is achieved only by playing out the play in hand while remaining detached enough to understand where the drama is and should be leading one. The real *telos* myth of Thomas More's *Utopia* is no *telos* at all; the utopian myth is important not in the ends it envisions but in the means it discloses by which man may mediate between his real and ideal worlds. It is the thrust of the disciplined conscience of the "self-conscious mind [remaining] negatively capable, alive to its own limits and to the world's good,"[10] seeking by the awareness of its ironic susceptibilities to aspire to, wish for, and embrace what is truly good and common and natural in the world that is More's final message in *Utopia* for the man aware of his social nature.

10. Berger, "The Renaissance Imagination," p. 63.

# List of Works Consulted

Adams, Robert P., "The Philosophic Unity of More's *Utopia,*" *Studies in Philology, 38* (1941), 45–65.

Allen, Ward, "Speculations on St. Thomas More's Use of Hesychius," *Philological Quarterly, 46* (April 1967), 156–66.

Andelson, R. V., "Where Society's Claim Stops," *American Journal of Economics and Sociology, 27* (January 1968), 41–53.

Aquinas, Thomas, *On the Governance of Rulers,* tr. G. B. Phelan, Toronto, 1935.

Augustine, *The City of God,* ed. Vernon J. Bourke, tr. Gerald S. Walsh, S.J., et al. (abridged), New York, 1958.

Barker, Arthur E., "Review Article: Clavis Moreana: The Yale Edition of Thomas More," *Journal of English and Germanic Philology, 65* (April 1966), 318–30.

Berger, Harry, Jr., "The Renaissance Imagination: Second World and Green World," *The Centennial Review, 9* (Winter 1965), 36–78.

Berneri, Marie Louise, *Journey Through Utopia,* Boston, 1951.

Bernstein, Michel, "Nouvelles Lumières sur l'*Utopie* de Thomas More," *Bibliothèque d'Humanisme et Renaissance, 24* (1962), 479–82.

Besant, Sir Walter, *London in the Time of the Tudors,* London, 1904.

Bindoff, S. T., *The Pelican History of England,* Vol. 5: *Tudor England,* Baltimore, 1963.

Bloomfield, Paul, *Imaginary Worlds,* London, 1932.

Bolgar, R. R., *The Classical Heritage and its Beneficiaries: from the Carolingian Age to the End of the Renaissance,* New York, 1964.

Bush, Douglas, *The Renaissance and English Humanism,* Toronto, 1939.

*Calendar of Letters, Despatches, and State Papers . . . Between England and Spain, Preserved . . . at Simancas and Elsewhere: 1483–1553,* ed. G. A. Bergenroth, 13 vols. London, 1862–1954.

Campbell, Lily B., "Tudor Conceptions of History and Tragedy in *A Mirrour for Magistrates,*" (Faculty research lecture at UCLA delivered May 9, 1935), Berkeley, 1936.

Cavendish, George, and William Roper, *Two Early Tudor Lives: The Life and Death of Cardinal Wolsey, George Cavendish: The Life of Sir Thomas More, William Roper,* ed. Richard S. Sylvester and David P. Harding, New Haven and London, 1964.

Chambers, R. W., *The Place of Thomas More in English Literature and History,* London, 1937.

———, *The Saga and Myth of Sir Thomas More,* London, 1928.

———, *Thomas More,* Ann Arbor, Mich., 1962.

Coulton, G. G., *Medieval Panorama: The English Scene from Conquest to Reformation,* Cleveland, Ohio and New York, 1964.

Crossett, John, "More and Seneca," *Philological Quarterly, 40* (October 1961), 577–80.

Davies, Gerald S., *Charterhouse in London,* London, 1921.

Dean, Leonard F., "Literary Problems in More's *Richard III,*" *PMLA, 58* (1943), 22–41.

Dickens, A. G., *Reformation and Society in Sixteenth-Century Europe,* New York and London, 1966.

Elyot, Thomas, *The Boke Named the Gouernour,* ed. H. H. S. Croft, 2 vols. London, 1883.

Erasmus, Charles J., *Man Takes Control: Cultural Development and American Aid,* Minneapolis, Minn., 1961.

Erasmus, Desiderius, *Christian Humanism and the Reformation: Desiderius Erasmus: Selected Writings,* ed. and tr. John C. Olin, New York, 1965.

————, *The Education of a Christian Prince,* tr. L. K. Born, New York, 1936.

————, *The Praise of Folly,* tr. H. H. Hudson, New York, 1941.

————, *Ten Colloquies,* tr. Craig R. Thompson, New York, 1957.

Fortescue, John, *The Governance of England,* ed. C. Plummer, Oxford, 1885.

Fowler, Elaine W., *English Sea Power in the Early Tudor Period* (Folger Booklets on Tudor and Stuart Civilization), Ithaca, 1965.

Frye, Northrup, "Varieties of Literary Utopias," *Daedalus, 94* (Spring 1965), 323–47.

Gayley, Charles Mills, *Plays of our Forefathers,* New York, 1907.

Giamatti, A. Bartlett, *The Earthly Paradise and the Renaissance Epic,* Princeton, 1966.

Gilmore, Myron P., *The World of Humanism: 1453–1517,* New York, 1962.

Harpsfield, Nicolas, *The Life and Death of Sir Thomas Moore,* ed. E. V. Hitchcock, London, 1932.

Heiserman, A. R., "Satire in *Utopia,*" *PMLA, 78* (1963), 163–74.

Hendriks, Dom Lawrence, *The London Charterhouse,* London, 1889.

Hexter, J. H., *More's "Utopia": The Biography of an Idea,* Princeton, 1952.

Hough, Lyn Harold, *The Christian Criticism of Life,* Nashville, 1941.

Huizinga, Johan, *The Waning of the Middle Ages,* New York, 1954.

Kaufman, M., *Utopias: or Schemes of Social Improvement,* London, 1879.

Laslett, Peter, *The World We Have Lost,* New York, 1965.

Liljegren, S. B., *Studies on the Origin and Early Tradition of English Utopian Fiction,* Uppsala, 1961.

Lucian, *Lucian,* tr. A. M. Harmon (Loeb Classical Library), 8 vols. London, 1913–.

Lupton, J. H., *A Life of John Colet,* London, 1909.

Mackie, J. D., *The Earlier Tudors: 1485–1558,* Oxford, 1952.

Maitland, Frederic W., *English Law and the Renaissance,* Cambridge, 1901.

———, and Francis C. Montague, *A Sketch of English Legal History,* ed. James F. Colby, New York and London, 1915.

Manuel, Frank E., "Toward a Psychological History of Utopias," *Daedalus, 94* (Spring 1965), 293–322.

Miller, Clarence H., "The English Translation in the Yale *Utopia:* Some Corrections," *Moreana, 9* (February 1966), 57–64.

Montague, Francis C. See Maitland.

More, Thomas, *The Correspondence of Sir Thomas More,* ed. E. F. Rogers, Princeton, 1947.

――――, *The English Works of Sir Thomas More Reproduced in Facsimile from William Rastell's Edition of 1557 and Edited with a Modern Version of the Same by W. E. Campbell,* 2 vols. London, 1931.

――――, *The Yale Edition of the Complete Works of St. Thomas More* (16 vols. New Haven and London, 1963――), vol. 2: *The History of King Richard III,* ed. Richard S. Sylvester; vol. 4: *Utopia, ed.* J. H. Hexter and Edward Surtz, S.J.

Morton, A. L., *The English Utopia,* London, 1952.

Mumford, Lewis, "Utopia, the City and the Machine," *Daedalus, 94* (Spring 1965), 271–92.

O'Grady, Walter, "A Note on Busleyden's Letter to Thomas More," *Moreana, 11* (September 1966), 33–38.

O'Sullivan, Richard, K.C., "Social Theories of St. Thomas More," *The Dublin Review, 199* (July to September 1936), 46–62.

Oswald, Arthur, *The London Charterhouse Restored* (reprinted from "Country Life"), London, 1959.

Phillips, Margaret Mann, *Erasmus and the Northern Renaissance,* New York, 1965.

Pico della Mirandola, Giovanni, *Oration on the Dignity of Man,* tr. A. Robert Caponigri, Chicago, 1956.

Plato, *The Republic,* tr. Francis MacDonald Cornford, New York and London, 1964.

Polak, Fred L., *The Image of the Future, 1,* Leyden, 1961.

*Quest for Utopia, The,* ed. Glenn Negley and J. Max Patrick, New York, 1952.

Roper, William, *The Lyfe of Sir Thomas Moore,* ed. E. V. Hitchcock, London, 1935. See also Cavendish.

Schoeck, R. J., "Thomas More, Lawyer and Judge," the

second of three *St. Thomas More Lectures* delivered at Yale University, Dec. 4, 1967.

Scott, James Brown, *The Spanish Origin of International Law: Francisco de Vitoria and His Law of Nations,* Oxford, 1934.

Seebhom, Frederic, *The Oxford Reformers,* London, 1887.

Sherwin, Proctor Fenn, *Some Sources of More's "Utopia,"* Albuquerque, N.M., 1894.

Sowards, J. K., "Some Factors in the Re-evaluation of Thomas More's *Utopia," Northwest Missouri State College Studies, 16* (June 1, 1952), 31–58.

Stapleton, Thomas, *The Life and Illustrious Martyrdom of Sir Thomas More,* tr. P. E. Hallett, London, 1928.

Surtz, Edward, S.J., *The Praise of Pleasure,* Cambridge, Mass., 1957.

————, *The Praise of Wisdom,* Chicago, 1957.

Sylvester, Richard S., text of a lecture delivered at a San Francisco symposium, Aug. 13, 1965 (to be published under the title "Detachment and Involvement in the World of Thomas More"), pp. 1–18.

Taylor, William F., *The Charterhouse of London,* London, 1912.

Thompson, E. Margaret, *The Carthusian Order in England,* London, 1930.

Vespucci, Amerigo, *Letter Concerning the Isles Newly Discovered in his Four Voyages,* tr. Bernard Quaritch, London, 1885.

# Index

Active life, 32n, 42, 45, 127–28, 134–35, 147–48
Adultery, as cause for divorce in Utopia, 107
Aesop, fable of philosophers in cave, 19n
Afterlife, belief in, 126. *See also* Punishment, divine; Virtue, and eternal reward
Agriculture: in England, 51–56; in Utopia, 76–77, 79, 84. *See also* Enclosure movement
Alaopolitans, war with Utopians and Nephelogetes, 114–15
Alienation, 45–48, 55–57, 58–59. *See also* Hythlodaeus, remoteness of
Allen, Ward, 142
Alliances. *See* Treaties
Amaurotum: meaning of name, 9, 10n; described, 77–83
Ambiguity: of Utopian institutions, 33, 75, 77, 82–90 passim, 95, 103–09 passim, 113, 120–21, 134–35; of the posture of defense, 92–95, 135–40. *See also* Irony, province of
Andelson, R. V., and paradox of utopian myth, 13–14, 24
Anecdote: of philosophers in cave, 18, 42, 63; of magnetic needle, 71–72; of incubation, 77, 84
Anemolian ambassadors, 47–48
Anemolius (Utopian poet laureate), 61n
Animals. *See* Butchery; Incubation; Sheep
Anydrus river, 9, 10n
Apprentices: in Utopia, 7n, 80, 82; in sixteenth century, 7n, 82
Aristotle: *Politics,* 64; on communism and lawsuits, 64–65
Armies. *See* War
Asceticism: and Utopian philosophy, 91, 127–28; and Utopian religion, 127–28. *See also* Pleasure; Religion
Audley, Sir Thomas, Lord Chancellor, 19n
Augury, 142

Barker, Arthur E., 126–27n
Baron, Hans, 32n
Beggars: and idleness, 55–56; absence of, in Utopia, 82
Berger, Harry, Jr.: three phases or moments, 2–3; green world, 3, 27; Latin *vs.* Greek, 5; Garden of Adonis, 10; liberty, 43, 148; and Morton, 50, 57

## DATE DUE

FEB 24 2011

GAYLORD                                    PRINTED IN U.S.A.